UNLEASHING THE ... RESILIENCE

# *IF SHE CAN,* **SO CAN YOU**

Lola Johnson-Owolabi

FIRST EDITION

ISBN: 978-1-7384132-0-1 (paperback)

If she can, so can you is published by TC Publishing

For information, please direct emails to: info@tc-publishing.com

TC PUBLISHING

# Content

*To my heavenly father, husband, son,*
*and every strong single parent out there.*

# Introduction

Have you ever looked at someone and wished that you could be like them? For example, when you were growing up, maybe at school, did you have a teacher who you really admired? Maybe it was the way they spoke, their confidence, the way they explained things or the way they dressed? Was there, amongst your friends, a certain girlfriend who stood out from the rest? Someone truly beautiful, poised, accomplished and popular? Admit it, did you even feel rather intimidated when you were around her?

I remember when I was in secondary school, a new girl, whom I will call KG, joined the class, during the middle of the term. KG was of mixed-race heritage, with long flowing hair, a great figure and a lovely face. Everybody, and I mean everybody, wanted to be her friend. She also had very wealthy parents and, as young impressionable schoolgirls, this endeared us to her further.

There have been a lot of studies carried out on what influences children's perception of beauty. One that I found interesting is by Juliana Buss and Tania Stoltz:

*Studies show that the standard of beauty that most people judge by are thinness, youth and proportionality. Beauty standards are present in society mostly through the influence of the media (soap operas, advertisements, magazines, films), family or institutional coexistence, beautification practices, gender relations, toys and literary stories. All these will contribute to the construction of bodies and identities of the subjects.*

*These patterns are not simple, natural or eternal, but have been constructed historically and culturally, ever changing and being reaffirmed by the media. The overvaluation of beauty by the media greatly affects children, especially girls, imposing desires in children and lining them up as prospective consumers.*

*Most studies about beauty and consumption are focused on adults, especially women, with only one article focusing on men. Even studies that highlight children, bring an adult discourse, highlighting the role of the media in the formation of children's perceptions. In other words, adults, in most texts, are talking about and for children.*

*In view of this, this study analyses children's perceptions of beauty standards, emphasising how these standards influence their lives and how they internalise according to age. The standards of beauty portrayed in the media, it seems, shape the imagination and even the speech of children. There is also a children's culture that has its own ideas about beauty standards, in which children are active subjects, but with different perceptions that are according to their age. It is also assumed that the older the child and the more inserted into the culture, the more the influence of beauty standards will affect him or her.*

When I moved to university, there was a young woman in our halls of residence who was breathtaking, with a near-perfect figure. She reminded me of Marilyn Monroe at the height of her fame. This woman was not only stunning but she also had an air of aloofness, which added to the mystery of who she was. She was very reserved, almost snobbish and belonged to the elite female club within the university. Funnily enough, I met her recently at a friend's 50th birthday, and yes – she is still beautiful!

Now, in adulthood, there are still women I admire, not necessarily for the same reasons I did when I was much younger – I will elaborate on this in later chapters. For now, I will say that when I was younger, I admired many people because of their outward appearance and what I believed to be their great looks, dress sense, style, material wealth, etc. As an adult, my perception has changed. It has been an arduous journey; however, I have now arrived at a place where I have accepted myself, my wide feet, my imperfections and all my foibles. I no longer want to be anyone else or live anyone else's life. Now, in all honesty, I can say that I would not want to swap anyone else's life for mine. I am pleased to say though, that there are still people I look up to and many people who have played a positive role in, and had an influence on my life.

I am a firm believer that no one is an island; we all need each other in the great jigsaw that is life and we must also realise that we are just as important a piece as anyone else.

This book has been years in the writing, through many stops and starts, and many personal battles. Now, I am finally able to put fingers to keyboard, although I have to confess that I originally started with a pen and notebook. It definitely has been a while!

The book, ***If She Can, So Can You***, is for all females, young and old, rich and poor. It's for every ethnicity, personality type and socio-economic background. No matter who you are, where you are from or your previous experiences – if there are still things you desire or wish to achieve, please do not despair. I can help you achieve those things, no matter how far-fetched you may feel they are. It is not a cliché, it is most definitely true, and the only person who can stand in the way of your heart's desires is YOU!

With respect to you, please believe me when I say that you are here for a reason. No man or woman was born without potential, without gifts or talent; no, not one of us. We are all on a journey of self-discovery.

You may not know what your gifts are yet and hopefully, there is still time for you to find out; absolutely no one was born empty. My question to you is, what will you do with the legacy of your life? Who will remember you? What will you leave behind?

My motto has always been my self-coined phrase: 'Think it, See it, Live it.' The mind is powerful, but it is important to learn how to dominate your mind with a positive conquering spirit. We are all too often embargoed by how we feel, yet it can only be our inner faith that determines how far we go in the journey of our life.

When I was about seven, I wanted to play the guitar. I loved singing and my siblings and I would sing along to the popular songs of the time in front of the mirror, hairbrushes in hand. My parents must have realised that I was musical; however, instead of the guitar I craved, they bought me a piano. I was pleased but it was not the same as a guitar. My love for music continued through school and today I can proudly say that I have completed two albums, written and produced my own music and have been the lead vocalist in various bands. My musical journey could be said to be the metamorphosis of my coaching journey.

Strangely, as much as I loved singing, I had no idea that I was any good and, looking back, I think I had pretty low self-esteem in this area. It was only when I got to university that a good friend of mine encouraged me to sing, telling me that I had a good voice and that I should use it. Thank God I listened to D, because with a boost to my confidence, I joined various university bands, took part in singing competitions and ended up gigging and singing my way through university. I often reflect on that period now and realise that if I did not have encouragement, I may never have been in a position to utilise my gift.

The same cannot be said of my longing to speak fluent French, however. It is one of my biggest regrets that I never achieved that fluency, but I have come to realise that neither age nor time can kill your desire or passion if you still want to achieve your goal badly enough. On the bright side, there is still time for me, and hopefully speaking French fluently will be something I can tick off my bucket list at some point.

The shy, retiring and reserved me still makes a rare appearance; however, she is no longer in control and definitely does not rule my life. She has given way to a bolder, more focused individual who is willing to take risks and plunge into the deep blue ocean. Maybe this is also your story: is it time for you to say goodbye to limiting belief and constant, perpetual fault-finding and embrace the powerful woman within? Enjoy the read and be inspired, transformed and renewed!

With love,

Lola.

# CHAPTER ONE
## *LETTING GO OF THE PAST*

*'Reflect upon your present blessings of which every man has many, not on your past misfortunes of which all men have some.'*

**- Charles Dickens**

Let it go, let it go! Let's face it, let he or she amongst us who does not have a past, cast the first stone! Everything that happens to you as an individual is important: the good, the bad and the indifferent. Yesterday's experience is tomorrow's teacher.

We have all made mistakes or let ourselves down in one way or another. Do you have an episode in your life of which you are thoroughly ashamed? Possibly there is a chapter in the story of your life that you wish you could erase? I thought so – you are not alone.

Life is full of choices, from small decisions like what to eat for dinner to much more significant things like choosing a career. All of us are faced with decisions to make on many things, large and small, every day.

Recently a study entitled 'What if?', conducted by One Poll, revealed that an astonishing number of people were unhappy with the way they lived their lives, either in the present or the past.

The survey of 2,000 British adults was commissioned by UK charity consortium 'Remember a Charity' and it showed that four out of ten people will readily admit that they regret how their lives have been lived so far. Devoting too much time to work and not spreading their wings and travelling more were amongst the most common regrets highlighted by the survey.

Other regrets that featured frequently were not looking after their health better and not spending more time with the family. Many people thought they could have been a better parent, of the survey respondents, forty per cent claimed afterwards that they now felt motivated to make positive changes in their life.

One thing that is very sure is that all of us will die one day, and most of us have no idea when that will be. Because time might be shorter than we think, it would be a terrible thing to reach the end of life with regrets. You might think that the results of the survey were a bit sad or bleak, but the fact that it prompted the people involved to think about changing their lives must be seen as a positive. It made the respondents think about those things they had always wanted to do but had always put off.

Many people are also concerned about leaving a positive legacy behind and worried about how they will be remembered by their children and other people they know. And when it came to how the survey participants wanted to be remembered, they were almost unanimous in wanting to be remembered as:

- talented
- sociable
- loving
- happy
- caring
- charitable.

Four in ten of the survey respondents were very keen to be remembered for being generous. Interestingly, however, when people were asked how they thought they would be remembered, they replied that they were more likely to be remembered for being anxious and moody!

Another big regret that was highlighted in the survey was the time that the respondents spent staring at screens of one sort or another, from smartphones to the TV – most thought they had spent too much time staring at these images. Another cause for regret was striving too much for financial success rather than focusing on more meaningful endeavours. The results of this survey are interesting and go to prove that we all have regrets – it's what we do about them that is important!

As I see it, the key issue is, how do we learn if the journey of life is void of challenges? Even fairy tales are a mixture of the good and bad, sadness before joy. It is often said that failure is not the person but the event.

Ladies, I am talking to you now: how many of you have ended up in a wrong relationship, or maybe you are in the wrong relationship right now? One that simply does not add any value to your life. Have you been there, walked that journey, or are you there now? Does it feel as though you are joined at the hip with someone who is more bad than good and who is crushing you physically and psychologically? Do you feel trapped and weighed down but also haunted by the thought that if you let your partner go, who else would want you?

How many hours have you spent daydreaming about your life and wishing that it was so much better? Maybe you wish you were in a loving relationship rather than the relationship that you are in that seems so unsatisfactory and unfulfilling? Do you really wish you were in a better financial position, or you were able to truly follow your desires? Maybe the dreams you have for yourself are ones in which you can escape the mundane or emigrate, to start a new and exciting life for yourself? Somehow, however, your feet are stuck firmly to the floor in what you know in your heart is a hopeless relationship, and you live day in, day out, chained to a life of mediocrity, just too afraid to step out of your comfort zone.

Maybe you are a lone parent, with your relationship having broken down, leaving you to fulfil the role of two people. When you are left without the support of a partner, with children, it can be a very lonely place. You may often feel alone and in despair. You may feel that you are completely trapped, unable to get out from under the responsibilities you have. You have been let down badly and it is really hard to see the light at the end of the tunnel. However desperate you feel and however hopeless your situation seems, it is important for you to realise that no situation has to be permanent and that life can definitely turn around. Those beautiful children are a blessing and they will appreciate the fact that you have sacrificed so much for them.

No matter the individual situation, each new day is an opportunity to start over. I know that it can sound a bit cliché, but life is a precious gift to be savoured, enjoyed and lived. As we wake up to each brand-new day, it's another opportunity to jump out of bed and exclaim, 'Thank God, I am still here!'

Now, I want you to take a moment to think about something. Have you ever wondered what the consequences would be to your family, friends and loved ones if you failed to rouse from your sleep in the morning? How that would affect everyone you know and love? It is a horrific thought, I know; however, it is also a reality that has happened and will happen to many people.

Living in the past is not adding much value to your life, and being stuck in the mud of the past can seriously damage your emotional health. Whatever has happened in the past should definitely not prevent you from moving towards a change of direction or to new beginnings. There may be people and events that seem to drag you back to the past, time and time again. But you need to make a conscious decision not to allow yourself to be dragged back to a time that has passed because, no matter what you do or what you wish, what is done is done, and you can't change what has already occurred. The present and the future are where your focus must lie. Bringing up the past every time you want to take a step forward, will just hold you back. So you failed previously? Join the club of millions across the globe who have also had false starts, disappointments and failures. The tabloids are full of stories of ordinary people and celebrities who have come unstuck in the past and had the spotlight shone on their past mistakes, publicised for all the world to see.

Have you ever considered what damage you could do to your future if you refuse to let go of the past? Believe me, that damage can be catastrophic. It can be compared to sinking in quicksand – the more you struggle to get free, the more the sand holds you in its grip. In the quicksand of the past, there will always be a way to break free. However, in this scenario, you need to grab hold of the rope of life and pull yourself up to safety.

The famous author Aldous Huxley said:

'If you have behaved badly, repent, make what amends you can, and address yourself to the task of behaving better next time. On no account brood over your wrongdoing. Rolling in the muck is not the best way of getting clean.'

Perhaps you are the one who has been wronged and left wounded and seething about past hurts. If that is the case, no matter how painful, hurtful or tragic the event or the memory, you need to progress with your life and let the situation go, however impossible that may seem. Regret and seething resentment are like a cancer that will eat away at you, so however hard it is to draw a line under past events and hurts, you have to do it for the sake of your future. Think of it this way: If you were to try to walk down the street looking over your shoulder all the time, instead of looking ahead, eventually you would fall over or crash into something. You need to have your eyes on the road ahead to keep moving forward.

Forgiveness may seem hard, but in the long run, it is so much easier than bitterness and resentment. Refusing to forgive may have far greater consequences than the pain of being wronged. Without forgiving, there can be no forgetting and the past hurt will always be there, like a heavy-weight, holding you back.

And then there is the harsh truth that not many people want to be around someone who is consumed by bitterness, resentment, malice and getting revenge. I can assure you that after a while, it will become very tiresome and draining no matter how much that person cares for you. Ms Vengeful will soon be off the list of invitees for parties and if that is you, you will soon find yourself being given a wide berth, with people dodging your invitations and always seeming to have something else to do when you suggest a meeting.

Then there are the actual physical effects that being unforgiving can have on the human body. Medical research has shown that there are many ways in which being unforgiving and resentful can affect the individual. These include:

- Muscle tensing, contributing to imbalances along the spine, with possible pain in the neck, back and limbs.
- Headaches that may occur due to increased tension of the neck muscles at the base of the skull.
- There may also be decreased blood flow to the joint surfaces due to the increased muscle tension around the joints.
- Blood flow to the heart may be constricted.
- Digestion may be impaired.
- Breathing patterns may change and become restricted.

The consequence of all of these physical effects makes it more difficult for the blood to remove waste from the tissues and reduces the flow of oxygen and nutrients to the body's cells. This can lead to an increased likelihood of inadequate tissue repair during sleep, impairing recovery from injury etc.

## 'The Heart of Healing'

Dr Guy Pettitt. MA, MSE (psych), MRCP, FRNZCGP, DOBS, RCOG.

*Being unforgiving has rightly been called the cancer of the soul, please don't let it eat you up, no one is worth putting yourself through so much anguish. Let the situation go, release yourself from the disappointment, failure, hurt, regret, wounded pride or whatever it is that grieves your heart. It is important to learn how to pick yourself up and start over.*

I have a philosophy in life, which is as follows: when you are digging for gold, it is not going to be easy. Gold is not found on the surface of the mine, it can be a difficult, treacherous and difficult job to unearth it. There may be many false starts, but to reap the reward of the discovery of gold, perseverance is vital. Searching for life's treasures is also difficult; it requires diligence, perseverance, tenacity and sheer determination.

Athletes train hard to win their medals; successful entrepreneurs have also experienced failure, bankruptcy and disappointment. One person's story, Thomas Edison, is inspirational. His story is of how many times he failed in his dream of inventing the electric light bulb and various other inventions. He had registered over 1000 patents; this was a man who experienced failure on a massive scale. The tide turned and 86 years after his death, his name is synonymous with the invention of the electric light bulb. In the 21st century, we are likely familiar with the Dyson vacuum cleaner,[and] the inventor, James Dyson, who also experienced heavy disappointment. He had previously failed to sell his invention to major manufacturers and proceeded to establish his own manufacturing company in June 1993. Now, 24 years later, he is now one of the richest men in the UK, with a net worth of US$4.9 billion. The lesser-known Mary Anderson also deserves full kudos for her invention of the windshield wipers; she was met with much scepticism on her invention in 1903. However, it is now safe to say that the windscreen wiper is a very useful invention and is mandatory for most vehicles.

There is rarely a success story which is devoid of struggle, pain, repeated failure and a myriad of other issues, either personal, professional or in business. The key point is that it's important not to dwell on these issues and as much as possible use them as a learning tool.

Recently, I was watching a BBC news programme. One of the interviewees was a general in the Afghanistan army. I listened with interest as he said, 'There are two words which are not in my dictionary, and they are "problem" and "fear".

This totally resonated with me, and not because I am totally fearless or problem-free. The general had been ambushed, shot at, subjected to numerous assaults and experienced more than his fair share of ill-treatment. However, he was resolved and determined that he would not give in to fear and problems. He would be invincible and likely equally determined and focused in his outlook and attitude to life and any negative onslaughts it brought. You may say, 'Well, he is a man and he's a general, how does that relate to me as a woman, who is not a general?'

My reply is that, as women, we can also take the same stand and adopt the same mindset. We all have the ability to refuse to allow anything in our past to hold us back.

## Time to reflect

Now, I would like you to answer these questions as honestly and fully as you can.

Is there anything you have done or had done to you that makes you uncomfortable and that you never seem able to forget? Be completely honest about what happened and why you feel the way you do.

1. Have you spoken to anyone about it and do you think it would help if you did?
2. When you think about the event from your past, write down, in a few words, what emotions come to the surface. What do you feel?
3. Have you got any ideas about how you can walk away from the negative and embrace more positive thoughts? Write down some ways in which you think you could overcome them.

## Tip

Don't let your past determine your future; keep your eyes focused ahead of you.

# CHAPTER TWO
## *DON'T PLAY THE VICTIM*

If we reflect upon our lives, we will all have had our share of bad luck, and we have all definitely faced times when things did not go as planned. Then there are the times when things seemed to spiral out of control, as though we were merely puppets at the end of strings pulled by others; when it seemed we were powerless to control our destiny. I am sure you can remember times that caused you a lot of grief, anger disappointment, hurt and bewilderment. It may have seemed, at times, as if you were having an out-of-body experience, looking down at yourself and your life as if you were merely an observer.

Maybe you have had your trust broken, or have suffered being physically, mentally or emotionally abused. Well, I am here to tell you, however harsh it may sound, that with the necessary counselling, therapy or spiritual exercise, the hurt you feel can dissipate, there *are* things that you can do, and they work!

*There is a useful website that has a lot of valuable information about dealing with and recovering from traumatic events.

The research states that a traumatic event can be defined as an experience that puts a person or someone close to them at serious risk of coming to serious harm or even dying. Something that could be described as a traumatic event might be:

- A road accident
- Violence/prolonged abuse
- Sexual attack or abuse
- A natural disaster
- A serious illness or the serious illness of a loved one
- The loss of a loved one.

So, what really happens to you when you experience something traumatic?

Here comes the science.

When you experience something traumatic, you will generate a stress response as a defence and that will lead to you feeling actual physical symptoms. Your behaviour might change, and you could experience strong emotions. This is what is described as the fight or flight response. In response to the trauma, your body produces chemicals, which is something it does naturally to prepare for any kind of emergency situation or event. This state of readiness can lead to physical symptoms such as:

- Increased blood pressure becomes raised
- Increased heart rate
- Increased sweating
- A loss of appetite caused by reduced activity within the stomach.

This might sound a bit alarming but these are perfectly normal reactions to any threat and they are designed to ready you to either fight or run away from the situation.

Shock and denial will often set in once the event is over. How quickly this feeling passes or rather, metamorphosises into anger, sadness or guilt varies. It could be within a few hours or it could be several days. In general, most people will begin to feel better and will gradually recover fairly quickly. However, problems arise when a person finds they fully work through and accept what has happened. This can give rise to more serious mental health problems, including depression or post-traumatic stress disorder (PTSD).

## Depression

Depression is very different from feeling sad or a bit down. When someone is truly suffering from depression, they may typically feel things like:

- Hopelessness
- Helplessness
- Intense anxiety
- Negativity.

They will, if they are truly depressed, find themselves unable to shake off such feelings; talking therapies like cognitive behavioural therapy (CBT) as well as counselling and psychotherapy can help, but often these patients require medication to help increase neurotransmitters that produce chemicals like serotonin and noradrenaline.

## Post-traumatic stress disorder (PTSD)

When people have PTSD, they will typically have feelings of anxiety that can persist for years, sometimes quite disproportional to the trauma that they suffered. People who have PTSD will often suffer from symptoms like:

- Feeling emotionally numb
- Anger

- Sleep disturbance
- Poor concentration
- Panic attacks
- Misuse of alcohol or drugs.

Probably the most successful treatment for PTSD will be talking therapies administered by a clinical psychologist. This kind of therapy involves a person being encouraged to talk about what happened in a lot of detail. Again, behavioural or cognitive therapeutic approaches are likely to be used. Antidepressants can also be given.

So, what should you do if you experience a traumatic event?

## Don't suffer in silence

If you have been through a traumatic event, there is no doubt that it can be difficult to talk to other people in the family or to friends. There can be many reasons for this – you may not want to cause your parent the trauma of knowing that you have been abused. However, it has been proven without doubt that sharing with people you trust will help you recover from the trauma. If there is no one that you think you can talk to, then there are a lot of organisations that will offer help.

## Take care of yourself

Following a traumatic event, self-care might feel insignificant or overwhelming. You may find little motivation to attend to basic personal hygiene or grooming. Yet, embracing routines and striving for a semblance of normalcy is crucial for recovery. Pay attention to your nutrition and avoid relying on alcohol or drugs as coping mechanisms. While they may offer temporary relief, they risk developing into harmful habits over time.

## Consider getting professional help

It takes a certain amount of swallowing our pride to reach out and ask for help. Maybe it would help to look at it this way: none of us are experts in everything, so it follows that everyone will need help at some time. If you need it, don't be afraid or embarrassed to ask.

When you have symptoms that are affecting your everyday life, then it might be time to seek professional help. Some of the symptoms you might experience that would make seeking professional help a good idea are:

- If you have no one to talk to
- If you are still feeling your initial symptoms six weeks after the trauma
- If someone whom you are close to says they think you need help
- If your study or work is suffering
- If you are finding it difficult to do mundane, everyday tasks
- If you have turned to alcohol or drugs to help you cope.

The first person you should go to for help and advice should be your family doctor or GP. They should be able to help by advising you on treatment and might also refer you to another professional locally. There are also voluntary organisations that are very good and will offer advice or a listening ear. One of those is the Samaritans, where you will find someone at the end of the phone twenty-four hours a day and who are fully confidential. There are others that your local surgery or a search of the internet should have a few suggestions.

Whatever has happened to you, it is important to try, as hard as it is, to put the pain behind you, even if you need help to do it. Do not allow the person responsible for your trauma to win by continuing to suffer. It is truly time to move on and not allow painful memories or a bad situation to dominate and dictate your life.

As humans, we are resilient, adaptable and flexible. We can adapt to different situations and it is very important for us to remember this. The old saying 'necessity is the mother of invention' is so true in day-to-day life.

I strongly believe that good can come out of bad, as well as the necessity to make lemonade when life gives you lemons. You can also grow stronger and turn the negatives in your life into positives. There are many charities and initiatives worldwide that have been established out of hurt, pain, misery and loss. They are doing great things to help ease the suffering of others.

We must determine our reaction when life throws us a curveball – it is similar to the concept of the glass half-full or half-empty scenario. We must not allow ourselves to wallow hopelessly in the mud of life for an indefinite period.

When I started writing this book, I was stuck at the Renaissance Hotel at LAX. I should have flown back to the UK several days earlier. However, due to the volcanic eruption in Iceland causing massive plumes of ash to cloud the skies, all flights were cancelled. I had to cancel so many meetings in the UK, and honestly, I can promise you, it is no fun when you are stuck in a place, no matter how glamorous it is, when all you want is to be at home. Friends said, 'Lola! You're in LA, make the most of it!'

Nothing they said made any difference. I just wanted to be at home. It was not fun being stuck in a country with little or no chance of getting out. It was rather like imprisonment, except that my cell was a very comfortable hotel room.

As I began to feel sorry for myself, it dawned on me that it could have been a whole lot worse. I was in a four-star hotel, I could come and go as I pleased. The hotel had a regular shuttle bus to LAX, which I could travel on to check the updates on flights back to London. They also had a regular shuttle to Manhattan Village Pier for shopping and food. If I got tired of hotel food, there was a fast-food restaurant across the street.

As I sat in the lobby writing, I truly began to count my blessings. There were thousands stranded across the world, just like me – some had probably run out of cash, maybe they had no accommodation or access to food. Indeed, I had seen many people camping out at the airports, some with children who should have been back at school. Maybe some had medical conditions, important assignments to fulfil or a myriad of other issues that needed to be attended to at their various destinations. That might have included possibly life-changing appointments. This really put things into perspective for me and I decided that there was no problem without a solution, even if the solution was a waiting game, dependant on when the volcano decided to cease spewing its ash.

I was not the only one in this situation and playing the victim would not improve the situation. That attitude only robs us of a good look. Wallowing in self-pity will definitely cloud judgement and any chance of a realistic perspective on the situation. Worse still, it may alienate us from the very people who could give us support.

On the subject of Los Angeles, heading back to my hotel, I passed the Los Angeles mission, which is very similar to the Salvation Army. I saw a long line of people queuing for a bed for the night. It reminded me of a similar scene in the Will Smith movie 'Pursuit of Happiness' where he portrayed Chris Gardner, a financial guru whose life story was told in the movie. We witnessed his story from his days of sheer desperation to the eventual triumph of his breakthrough. Chris Gardner endured poverty, humiliation, rejection, shame, family breakdown and the uncertainty of homelessness. What I admired most in the movie was that he did not once wallow in the mud of rejection; he stayed strong for his son and was determined to persevere. I guess that's why a movie was made about his life. The movie is an inspirational one and if you have not seen it, I highly recommend it. As the old adage says, *'What does not kill you, makes you stronger!'*

Jane Tomlinson, who eventually succumbed to cancer in September 2007, was a great example of the strength of the human spirit. She was a gutsy lady who refused to allow her cancer diagnosis to subdue her. She kept on competing in sport, fighting and resisting. Without a doubt, she put up the most spirited fight. Along her journey, she raised almost £2 million for charity, ran marathons and collected a CBE. It is testament to her legacy that I am writing about her several years after her passing.

I know that we are all different; however, resilience is such a powerful trait to possess. When life brings any kind of misfortune to your door, there are many different strategies you can adopt to deal with it. You could simply roll over and let the situation wash over you, or you could put on your boxing gloves and fight back. I hope you decide to do the latter. Crying, screaming and shouting may give you some temporary relief, but in the long term, stronger action is required.

In short, if you have been given a life-threatening diagnosis (God forbid), the truth is that you do not have to accept it without a fight; you can fight as much as you are able to. You do not have to roll over and let the situation squeeze the life out of you. A positive mindset is so important and you will need it to tackle the vicissitudes of life.

I sometimes practise cognitive behavioural coaching on myself. In the past, I used to really catastrophise situations. If I was late for a meeting, for instance, I would be so worried and stressed. Now, I am at the stage in my life where I know that worrying and stressing cannot change the situation and I condition my mind to stress less about issues which are out of my control.

A positive mindset may help you feel better about yourself and the event, and it is important to note that fear is a negative emotion. It is little wonder that it is also known by the acronym 'False Expectations Appearing Real'.

I remember watching Sky News and a story that featured a blind skier. I was totally amazed by this man, who had been paralysed by fear in his life but was now participating in one of the most dangerous sports. After watching him, I thought to myself, how could I allow anything to hinder me in my journey towards my destiny? I almost felt like I needed to wake up and live. I am sure we all have our determination points, and this was mine.

As women, we are emotional beings and we sometimes express ourselves through tears and crying, and that can sometimes be therapeutic. I have shed many tears of both joy and sorrow in my lifetime. Tears are not a sign of weakness but after the tears have been dried must come the change of mindset and a call for action. Sometimes it can be easy to fall into playing the blame game, dropping the reason for your issues at the door of others. It may also be easier to take the speck out of someone else's eye than to remove the log in yours. It is more comfortable to look outward than to reflect inwards. However, as hard and brash as it may sound, we need to get over ourselves and move forward. We should not be ruled by our feelings, but we do need to be moved by our faith in ourselves and a better tomorrow. What is there to gain by blaming everyone else for life's mishaps?

## Question time

1. Can you reflect on a time when you have empowered someone? How did it make you feel?
2. Think of things that you could do to move forward and let go of the past.
3. What can you do to take on more responsibility in your life and relationships?

## Tip

Change your stance and mindset to allow yourself to move in a more positive direction.

# CHAPTER THREE
## FINDING HELP WHEN YOU NEED IT

*'We are each of us angels with only one wing, and we can only fly by embracing one another.'*

**- Luciano de Crescenzo**

Sometimes we have to go through life's challenges, battles and disappointments by ourselves. However, there is truth in the old saying that a problem shared is a problem halved. No individual has all of the answers to life's questions and it is a privilege to share your issues with someone you can lean on, confide in and who will not betray your confidence.

At the moment your confidante may be your partner, a sibling, best friend, a parent, even your child. Whoever it is, I am sure you agree that once you have relieved yourself of the burden by sharing, you are likely to feel much better. This may happen even if your confidante is not able to give you any practical advice; the fact that someone is listening and taking time to support you emotionally goes a long way to relieving the burden, although you do need to be talking to the right person.

Some people will seek professional help when they are in despair while others will lean on friends or family. It's a personal choice and you have to be comfortable with the choice you make or there may be no benefit to you at all. We are all different and even the most private of people may find that therapy can be very useful.

## What is therapy?

According to Wikipedia, therapy (or treatment) is the attempted mediation of a health problem, usually following a diagnosis in the medical field. It is synonymous with the word 'treatment' among psychologists, and the term may refer specifically to psychotherapy or talk therapy.

In a past advert, telecommunications giant British Telecommunications (BT) claimed that 'it is good to talk'. This is an area in which I find myself agreeing with them, and there is an emphasis at this moment on talking more and catching up rather than texting. You may agree or disagree with me, but it really does seem as though we don't talk as much as we used to – we email, we text, we WhatsApp, we are on Instagram, Snapchat and a host of other platforms, but have we lost the art of talking as a result? I would be the first to admit that I love privacy and I am very comfortable with my own company, but I also really like to talk when I am in a chatty mood.

One of the most recommended types of therapy is talk therapy.

Suzanne La Combe, 2007, (CEDR, Psych), defined counselling as:

Helping with problems in living, through interaction with a trained professional.

- Offering a way to gain perspective on your emotions, behaviour and relationships.
- Providing a means to express your feelings and identify patterns of thinking.
- Alleviating anxiety, depression and anger in their many forms.

- Helping to develop communication skills for dealing with conflict and frustration.
- A means for addressing pain, working through loss and adding meaning to life.

Counselling can be described as a way to be empowered. I would always recommend counselling or talk therapy as a way forward for people who are quite vulnerable and courageous in facing their fears etc. and actively seeking help. Maybe they want more from their lives and are either seeking expansion or fulfilment.

## Benefits of talk therapy

Talk therapy helps all sorts of people in many different situations. Other names for talk therapy might be counselling, which we have already mentioned, psychological therapies or talking treatments.

Anybody who is going through a particularly hard time or has emotional issues that they really need help with will benefit from talk therapy. In fact, for a lot of adults who are depressed, it has been found to be more effective than taking medication. One type of talk therapy – cognitive behavioural therapy (CBT) – is even available on the NHS. If you do ever feel that you are in need of this kind of therapy, it might be useful to know that you can refer yourself to an NHS psychological therapy service directly, without going through your GP for the referral. You may also find a list of accredited and approved therapists at your GP surgery. It is also worth noting that if you get a referral from your GP, you will probably have to wait a few weeks before you get to see a therapist, and you probably will not have a lot of choice about who you see.

## How talk therapy can help

I've talked about confiding in relatives and in friends, and for most of us, that will be something we are happy to do and will get great benefit from. However, there are those of us for whom, or certain occasions in which, it is easier to talk with a stranger about the problem we have, rather than to somebody who knows us. When you go for therapy, a therapist or trained counsellor will listen to what you tell them about what is troubling you and then help you to find the answers and a way forward with your problems. They will not tell you what to do and they will not judge you.

When you see your therapist or counsellor, you will be able to cry, talk or even shout out loud, or just sit in contemplative silence. The benefit of talking to a counsellor rather than a relative or friend is that they don't know you and are not emotionally involved with you, so they will not have their own agenda to add to the issues that you're facing. Your therapist will be able to help you see things differently and will listen to what you say and always respect you and your opinions. Sessions with therapists will usually be one-to-one, but can also be held in group sessions or, in the case of relationship counselling, couples. Counselling would normally be conducted face-to-face, but since the days of COVID-related restrictions, it's now common for sessions to be held using Skype, Zoom, phone or even email.

There are many different forms of talk therapy, but all have one thing in common: they all aim to make you feel better. Typically, people will say that although talk therapy can't make their problems disappear, this type of therapy makes it a lot easier for them to cope and feel better about themselves. People will go for talk therapy for different reasons such as:

- Anxiety
- Depression

- Phobias
- Eating disorders
- Coping with addiction
- Coping with trauma
- Coping with abusive relationships.

Talk therapy is also often used for people who have serious mental health conditions such as bipolar disorder or schizophrenia, and can also be used alongside medication.

## When the going gets tough

When times are really tough and you find yourself at your lowest ebb, you can do the things that we've already talked about, such as speaking to a trusted friend or relative and reading this book to show you how to find, hold on to and develop your resilience. But it is also very true that you could be helped to cope by talk therapy.

Perhaps you are emerging from an abusive relationship, with your self-confidence on the floor, or maybe you have lost someone very dear to you through illness. It could be that you've lost your job and have no idea how you are going to survive financially. Maybe you've been told that your hopes of having a family are very remote and you're trying to come to terms with the fact that you're going to have to deal with infertility. There are many different reasons that people get depressed or feel desperate and, as I've already said, the only thing you need to remember if you find yourself in that position, is that there is help for you out there, in one form or another. You just need to reach out for it.

It would surprise nobody to know that people who suffer from long-term health conditions are likely to suffer from depression; if you find yourself in that position, then talk therapy has a proven track record.

There are some very common illnesses that have been shown to benefit greatly from talk therapy. These include:

- Multiple sclerosis
- Diabetes
- Cancer
- Stroke
- Heart disease
- Chronic lower back pain (when talk therapy will often be combined with specially designed exercise).

The great thing about talk therapy is that it can be adapted to any group of people; for instance, people in older age groups who may be suffering from loneliness or have lost a partner and are particularly prone to depression.

## Past abuse and talk therapy

People, particularly women who have been sexually or physically abused or people who have experienced racial discrimination, find talk therapy helpful. Especially where women are concerned, sometimes the real horror of a situation that they've been in is not something they feel they can divulge in its entirety to a friend or relative. This is where talk therapy becomes very important, giving the person who has suffered abuse the ability to speak freely and really address all the issues that they need to.

## Relationship problems and talk therapy

These days, it can be easy to assume, but people do give up on relationships too easily. They throw in the towel and move on to the next relationship without really doing all they can to save the relationship that they're in. Talk therapy can help couples whose relationships are in trouble. If you find yourself in this position, it's worth a try to see if you can get things back on track. If not, then talk therapy can be a great support through a separation and even through eventual divorce. Obviously, couples therapy is aimed at people being seen together but even on your own, there is a lot of help that you can get with this particular type of therapy.

## Family talk therapy

As women, we always have something to worry about. If you have been continually worried over the behaviour of your child or children, or you're finding family life intolerable, there is even talk therapy for families. This is another adaptation and a very useful one that can address specific family problems like helping children cope with divorce or the break-up of a relationship, especially if there's been abuse or other traumatic events involved. This can also be very helpful when children are suffering from eating disorders or other issues such as gaming or screen time addiction.

## Anger management

This is a really useful type of talk therapy which has helped many people step back from the brink. If you have anger issues yourself, or if you are living with a partner who has anger issues, it can be very helpful to see a talk therapist who specialises in dealing with such issues.

Of course, therapy and counselling are not the only solutions, but talking, either as part of therapy or to a trusted friend, may help. Some people, when they are under stress, will even talk to themselves!

I find that prayer works for me in much the same way as meditation and other spiritual exercises work for others. Whenever I am worried, anxious, indecisive, uncertain and fearful, I pray. It provides me with relief and comfort and I have been engaging in prayer for many years.

In a world where many people don't have any sort of religion, I am not ashamed to declare that prayer works for me; it helps me and is a source of comfort. It can be done alone or with others. The message might be 'I need your help', 'save me' or 'why me?' It might be 'I'm tired. I don't know what to do'. Prayer, in my opinion, is also communication. It is just that the person you are engaging with is not physically in the room.

Now I want to talk about coaching.

## What is coaching?

My definition of coaching is 'purposeful assistance guiding possible change', but coaching is one of those professions where each practitioner has a different definition based upon their personal perspective and journey.

The dictionary describes coaching as a recognised discipline engaged by many professionals involved in human development and focused on achieving results.

Having coached others and also having had the opportunity to be coached myself, I have also found that coaching sometimes consists of being given a push in the right direction to help you stay on track on the journey to your outcomes.

Coaching is often intertwined with mentoring, and both are worthy of pursuit. The fact of the matter is that life, as we know it, cannot be navigated on our own. It is rare that someone is so self-contained that they will never need anyone to lean on.

There's that old saying which states that if you want to go on a long journey, take someone with you! Life is like a relay race, you constantly need someone waiting in the wings to take the baton from you.

Coaching may be a good learning intervention if you are able to find the right one. Be picky when choosing a coach. Chemistry is really important when it comes to getting the best out of coaching because it is hard to imagine being fired up and filled with inspiration if the person who is coaching you has not gained your trust and is not on the same wavelength as you are.

A good coach should not tell you what to do but should, by probing carefully and questioning you, get you to look within yourself and find the answers to the issues that you are trying to address.

A good coach should work with you to help you see the way forward for yourself. A skilled coach will be worth their weight in gold. That is not to say that all the effort should come from your coach – oh no, that's not how it works! To get the best from coaching, you will also need to pull your weight, as part of the coaching process.

Mentoring is slightly different, although, as previously mentioned, the boundaries between the two disciplines may often overlap. For example, as a qualified coach, I sometimes find myself in mentoring mode. 'What is the difference?' I hear you ask.

It is interesting that the Cambridge English Dictionary describes a mentor as 'a person who gives a younger or less experienced person help and advice over a period of time, especially at work or school'.

I would add to this that it can also involve showing, telling, directing and advising a person. In both coaching and counselling, the person being coached or counselled should have an opportunity to talk and the professional should hopefully listen more and talk less. For a coach, being able to listen might be their biggest asset, as understanding the person they are coaching is always going to be vital for the best result. A counsellor should not tell the person they are counselling what to do; again, listening skills will be what will help most.

Sir Richard Branson, who has had a hugely successful career, said on the subject of mentoring: 'Going it alone is an admirable but foolhardy and highly flawed approach to taking on the world.' I totally agree that no man is an island – can you name anyone who has achieved greatness by doing it all on their own?

I know how important it is to seek help when you need it. The choice to ask for help is definitely in your hands. What you should not do, however, is wallow in whatever situation you may find yourself in. It may not even be a negative situation; it may be that you just need help with your direction in life, and one thing that I can promise you is that there is definitely someone out there who has walked your path, whose journey mirrors your own and who has felt your pain. There is also someone out there who can help you and would love to do so. There is someone out there who understands exactly what you are going through, and you know who that is. Why don't you seek the help you need today? Make that call!

## Time to reflect

1. Think about where you are in your life right now. Could you benefit from a coach, mentor or therapist? Identify the things you need help with and write them down.
2. Think about the type of help that you need. Write down the way that the service would help you and support you in fulfilling your life's goals.
3. Think about the help you need and why you need it. Then identify where you will go for that help. Who will you approach? Are you ready to make a conscious effort to get the necessary help you require, and if so, when?

## Tip

No man is an island, we all need someone to lean on – two is better than one!

# CHAPTER FOUR
## EDUCATE AND DEVELOP YOURSELF

*'Wisdom outweighs any wealth.'*

**- Sophocles**

No matter how skilled or gifted you are, there is always room for improvement. I am a great advocate of honing your skills and improving upon existing knowledge, skill set and experience. Robert Cushing sums it up when he says, *'The fact is, that to do anything in the world worth doing, we must not stand back, shivering and thinking of the cold and danger, but jump in and scramble through as well as we can.'*

How many times have we heard the words, 'What is worth doing, is worth doing well. If not, do not bother'? You must also have heard that 'failing to plan is planning to fail'. Like it or not, clichéd or not, it is true. Take a look at this world of ever-increasing competition – ordinary just won't do and it is important to strive to become an expert in your chosen field. That is why whatever is worth doing is worth doing well. Of course, it takes motivation and inspiration, but you must try and find the will to succeed in your chosen field.

I know that millions are in jobs and even professions that they absolutely hate. So, if you are doing something that puts a spring in your step as you jump out of bed each morning, then you are truly blessed. I understand that it is difficult to be motivated if you are bored and uninspired, but this may be the kick-start you require to truly follow your dreams. Fulfilment in your journey is key; life is just too short to be stuck in a dead-end job or unfulfilling profession. Education and acquired knowledge may be the key you need to break the vicious cycle of an uninspired life.

I remember a caterer I met at a 50th birthday celebration at the Hilton Hotel in Central London. It was a great gathering, the menu had an Afro-Caribbean theme and the food was very tasty. As something of a gourmet, I much prefer the simplicity of a Coke and a packet of crisps over a meal that's dull and tasteless.

So there I was, enjoying the ambience of the party when I noticed the caterer directing the staff. I was very impressed with his poise and authority. He was extremely hands-on. I decided to have a word, especially as I was also planning an event and I knew, without a second thought, that I could trust at least that part of my event to someone like him, implicitly.

The caterer and I got talking. I was more impressed now, not only with the food and menu but also because the caterer told me that he had decided to become an expert in his field by studying for an MBA to gain the knowledge he needed to develop his business.

That got me thinking about talent and made me realise that it is simply not enough to have talent in a particular area without anything to back it up. Take the top fashion houses, for example. They could not have survived and enjoyed their longevity without a team of business savvy professionals, including accountants, brand specialists, marketing executives, designers and tailors all working behind the scenes.

It is rather like the analogy of a swan gliding effortlessly across the water. What we don't see are the legs paddling frantically, working hard under the water. The creative product will always need much more than just that serene gliding talent to be a success.

You may not be at the stage in your career or business where you can afford to have a team of experts in your corner, but even if you're a one-woman band, you can be determined to become an expert or broaden your horizons. You can be determined to learn more and if your strengths are on the creative side, you might want to hone your skills on the business side. No knowledge is ever lost; even if it is not needed immediately, you can store it up for the future.

My conversation with that caterer brought home to me again the fact that talent may never be enough. Talent needs to work hand in hand with experience, knowledge, education, development, wisdom and understanding. It is because of this that a mentor, a coach or a consultant may be important and key to your particular business survival. Success is all about a holistic approach.

So my caterer, armed with the MBA, was determined that he would not be an ordinary caterer. The horizon was now broadened and, with his acquired business acumen, he decided to approach premium hotels such as the Hilton, Marriott and Ramada to see if their venues and kitchens could be hired when he needed them. This worked well as the caterer worked within a niche market of Afro-Caribbean cuisine. It was also important for hotels' clientele as they were mainly ethnic minorities who preferred their ethnic cuisine for weddings, parties, conferences, etc. The long and short of this is that he was able to tick the boxes and keep his clients happy – and keep them coming back to him.

I was intrigued because I had always thought it was not possible to bring in outside food to hotels or restaurants and that, as a guest, you would have to choose from the menu that they were offering. Here was a man who had completely changed the game plan by operating in a niche market, bringing an ethnic menu to the table and doing it all in the plush surroundings of top hotels, and with their blessing! That is what you call thinking outside the box. And there were elements of his story that resonated with my own.

My personal experience in my journey of knowledge was similar. I have always had an interest in fashion and accessories and, more often than not, I will get compliments about something that I am wearing. So, with my extensive travels around the world, I kept my eyes open for things that seemed unique and beautiful, stylish or just plain irresistible. I started selling a few of the bits and pieces that I discovered on my travels and it was really going very well. I have always been a person who is looking one step ahead and so my next thought was that I should open a shop.

However, before I did this, I did a couple of test runs and a pre-launch weekend. The takings were very encouraging. That was not enough for me, however, and I realised that I needed to know more about the inner workings of a retail fashion business. I was excited about the chance to sell the things I loved to people who would truly appreciate them, but I did not allow myself to get carried away. I realised that you could never know enough about something from the periphery and that I would have to know how it all worked from the inside out to really appreciate what was involved. I enrolled on a few courses at the London College of Fashion. Initially, I embarked on a six-week course entitled 'How to Start Your Own Fashion Retail Business' and what an eye-opener it was! I could not believe how valuable the knowledge from that course was. I learnt so much and met like-minded individuals with whom I could share ideas, knowledge and wisdom. I had not been attending very long before I realised that I was not ready to open the shop. It was a disappointment, but I pushed my plans back and estimated that it would take me a full year before I was ready to take that step.

I realised that I needed to be realistic with my plans. Remember that old faithful saying – 'When you fail to plan, you plan to fail'? I did not want that to be my fate and, looking back now, it was the best decision I could have made.

It did take me a year before I was ready to open the boutique. I hate to think what might have happened if I had given in to my first spontaneous urge to open the year before. There is no doubt in my mind that I would have found it a struggle from the outset without the extra study and work that I had done. The retail business is competitive and it is hard enough for even experienced merchants to succeed, so if you add inexperience and a lack of understanding to the mix, I am sure that the result would have been a total disaster.

The knowledge and insight I gained through attending the fashion course helped my understanding of the fashion industry no end and it led to other courses at the college. I know that those courses were crucially important to get me the extra insight and information I needed to embark on my journey into the fashion industry.

One of the most useful lessons I learnt on the course, and one that I calculated ended up saving me thousands of pounds, was to look carefully at all possible choices of venues for a shop. When we think about a retail venue we will naturally think 'shop'. However, the course lecturer advised that people who were considering a future in retail should think about alternative venues such as a market stall to begin with and could also make enquiries with the local council that may have some retail space for rent. This, for me, was such valuable advice because, with those words ringing in my ears, I went on to find retail space off the famous Baker Street, rented from Westminster Council for fifty per cent less than a private landlord was asking for similar premises on the same street!

I have always thought that timing is everything. That said, opening the boutique in the middle of a recession was a challenge. But opening my first boutique is an achievement of which I am extremely proud. People liked what I had to offer and it was a great validation that so many people seemed to have the same taste as me. I received many glowing reviews from clients and enjoyed selling my pieces and interacting with the public throughout the time that I had my shop. I eventually closed the boutique so that I could focus on my coaching career.

When eventually, with a lump in my throat, I closed the door of the boutique for the last time, I remember my younger sister saying, 'At least you did it!' And I had done it! But it was time to move on.

## Education or experience in the marketplace cannot be bought

The importance of education or personal development in any field, even just in life, cannot be underestimated. The world is constantly evolving and advances in technology are being introduced and updated almost hourly.

An article entitled 'Thought-provoking discussion from the Royal Geographical Society' discusses some of the challenges of keeping pace with digital evolution in the twenty-first century, and I would like to share an interesting fact with you.

- The memory capacity and speed of computers DOUBLE every 18 months (according to Moore's Law).

*Moore's law is a technological trend which states that the number of transistors created in an optimal minimum cost, doubles every 18-20 months. This means that the processing power of computers doubles every 18-20 months, or the price of the same processing power halves. This results in what is known as 'exponential growth'.*

*It was conceived by Gordon Moore, who was in charge of Intel in the 1960s. It describes the exponential growth in computing power that enables the average mobile phone to process instructions millions of times faster than the earliest computers.*

## The challenge

The internet is evolving rapidly and plays a central societal role in transforming cultural, economic, social and political landscapes. The benefits are self-evident, but are societies equipped to keep pace with the consequences of our increasing reliance on this technology?

Here are some timeline facts from that article, which certainly made me think.

**1969:** ARPANET, the first computer network the world had ever seen, was conceived by the American Pentagon's Defence Advanced Research Projects Agency (DARPA).

**1971:** The first email was sent by an employee at technology company BBN, Ray Tomlinson, who decided to use the @ symbol to separate his username from the name of his computer.

**1971:** There were 2,300 transistors on a single microchip. Thirty years later, in 2011, engineers were able to fit 2.9 billion transistors on each microchip.

**1991:** On 6 August, Sir Tim Berners-Lee created the World Wide Web. At the time he was working at the European particle physics laboratory at CERN, Switzerland.

**1995:** Six million online users are recorded.

**2005:** One billion estimated users of the web are recorded.

Source: Internet World Stats, January 2012.

The situation was changing all the time and by 2012, the number of Internet users globally stood at:

Asia – 1 billion

Europe – 500.7 million

North America – 273 million

L America/Carib. – 235.8 million

Africa – 139.8 million

Middle East – 77 million

Oceania/Australia – 23.9 million.

In 1990, things were different. These were the top ten countries and number of users in each of those countries:

1. United States: 1,981,674
2. Canada: 99,970
3. Australia: 99,709
4. Germany: 99,604
5. Sweden: 50,050
6. Netherlands: 50,043
7. UK: 49,953
8. Switzerland: 39,763
9. France: 30,063
10. Norway: 30,041

By 2019, both the country mix and number of users had changed again, this time quite dramatically.

1. China: 840,080,566 (58.80%)
2. India: 627,000,000 (46.83%)
3. United States: 244,090,854 (75.23%)
4. Brazil: 141,206,801 (67.47%)
5. Japan: 115,845,120 (90.87%)
6. Russia: 109,446,612 (76.01%)
7. Indonesia: 85,242,816 (32.29%)

8. Mexico: 82,470,752 (63.85%)
9. Germany: 69,304,405 (84.40%)
10. Philippines: 63,003,313 (60.05%)

Source: https://businessfibre.co.uk/top-10-internet-users/

A glance at these facts and figures should convince you of the need to keep up to speed.

In the developed world, there is so much opportunity for learning: evening classes, online courses, short courses, adult education covering everything from taxidermy to applied mathematics, they are all there, for anyone who takes the time to find them.

I often say that the brain is like a stomach – the more you fill it, the more it stretches and the more it craves. Life offers a whole array of opportunities to be developed and empowered and as harsh as it may sound, there is no excuse for remaining ignorant in this ever-changing world. Think of yourself as a surfer; if you don't keep on top of the wave, you will be plunged into the depths.

With imagination, hobbies can become income streams and passions can become profitable – it all depends on the imagination and the determination of the individual. In almost every town and city in the UK, you will find libraries where you can borrow books, read newspapers, look up journals and browse the Internet. There might be a hundred different reasons to put it off: the kids, the partner, the job. However, if you are truthful, what may stop you could be the elephants in the room, namely distractions, laziness and procrastination. The only way to overcome these issues is through sheer willpower and determination. I have experience in this area as I had to grapple with and conquer them all in order to get this book out! I had to evict them from my mindset. And therein lay the solution – my mindset had to change and I just had to get on with writing, and that, dear reader, is why you are reading my book today.

The human spirit is extremely resilient. It is absolutely amazing, in fact, what the human spirit and the human body can cope with. Despite our weaknesses, if we want to fulfil a particular goal or achieve a particular outcome badly enough, we can. Education and personal development open doors which ignorance keeps firmly closed. We have all heard the saying that 'knowledge is power'; to this, I would like to add that 'ignorance is weakness'. Education and personal development do not only add value to your life and well-being, but they can also open doors to greater opportunities which can earn you success, self-respect, accolades, prosperity and breakthroughs along the way.

What I love about living in the twenty-first century is the fact that you no longer need to be specifically academic to make a success out of life. When I was in school (many years ago), there was a great emphasis on intelligence quotient and academic excellence. It is not that academic attainment is no longer important, it is, and more and more people are attending university, even though it is now expensive to do so. What is important to note is that the world is now recognising other forms of intelligence and flair, as identified by Howard Gardner of Harvard in his book *Frames of Mind: The Theory of Multiple Intelligences* (1983). These are described as follows:

- Visual-Spatial – picture, graphic/artistic skills; mental imagery smart
- Naturalist – animals and plants; nature smart
- Musical – sound/music rhythm; tone and pitch smart
- Logical – numbers/numerical reasoning, calculations; mathematical smart
- Existential – life and human existence smart
- Interpersonal – people empathy/sensitivity; human relationship smart

- Bodily-kinaesthetic – body, physical and object manipulation smart
- Linguistic – word, language, reading; writing smart
- Intra-personal – self-awareness/understanding; feeling smart.

This is fascinating information. Can you identify your strengths from within the list? Although not everyone agrees with Gardner's theory, one thing cannot be disputed and that is within this list, we will all have our weaknesses, strengths and areas for further development. Can you imagine if David Beckham's parents had discouraged him from playing football and instead encouraged him to focus on being an accountant? If they had then we may have never heard of him. It is obvious that from an early age, he had a natural ability towards the bodily-kinaesthetic (kinaesthetic intelligence) and his skills were further honed by practice and opportunity. However, even he had to make an effort with self-improvement – anyone who is successful has walked this path. Beckham has reaped the fruits of his labour and achieved worldwide fame because he followed the path that his unique talents led him down.

Sometimes we do not always get the opportunities we need at the particular time we need them, but it's still a good idea to keep trying. An inspirational book I read encourages us 'that whatever your hands find to do, then do it well'. Talent, gifts and potential are important but it is also important to develop skills and hone the talent, just as a naturally gifted singer embarks on voice lessons and training to develop their voice and possibly improve breathing techniques and vocal ability as well. No matter how great the talent in whatsoever discipline, it still needs to be recognised, nurtured, honed, developed, refined – the list is endless!

In my spare time, I sing and to my credit, I have released two albums, not because I wanted any form of fame, but simply because I love singing and music, especially jazz. I think I have an above-average voice;

however, I know now, having not had a single music lesson, that if I had developed my voice and learnt to play the guitar as I had wanted to when I was a child, I would most likely have been a much better and a more technical singer today.

So there you have it! Your passion, your gifts and talents can sometimes be turned into profitable gain, but your God-given gift may not be enough and it is very likely that it will require a great deal of hard work, discipline, sacrifice, resilience and a lot of self-motivation to truly make a difference and get noticed.

## Question time

1. When did you last attend a training or personal development course?
2. How have you applied what you learnt in your home, career or business?
3. What course do you think would benefit your own development in the near future?

## Tip

The brain has never burst because it has too much information contained within it.

# CHAPTER FIVE
## DECLUTTER THE JUNK AND RENEW YOUR MINDSET

Hold it – I can almost hear you saying, 'I am really scared to start my own business, how will I deal with the tax man and employees, how can I give up my salary and take such a great leap of faith?' I can also hear that little voice that whispers continually in your ear, 'Who is going to buy my products and where will I sell them?' I know because I have stood on that threshold myself.

Fear and procrastination are very powerful enemies, but they do not have to be. It has taken me some time, but I know now that if you do not fulfil your own dreams then you will likely only be able to fulfil the dreams of someone else, your employer for instance. This is not a clarion call to get you to give up your job and go do whatever. This is a cry to all those who truly want to become their own boss, those who have toyed with the idea and know that they are sick and tired of being in the same position, answerable to someone else. This is for those with a gift and talent or a business idea that the world needs to see and hear. Maybe this is for you and maybe it's not, but if you recognise yourself, please take note as this is my passionate plea to you.

It is a feeling that most of us will be familiar with; we have an interview to attend or a talk to give and we're feeling the pressure. There's a lot at stake and it's very important that we do well. Our human nature is feeling the strain – are we going to sink or swim?

Naturally, the field of psychology has an awful lot to say about how our human nature has adapted us to be able to cope with pressure when that pressure is chronic. Perhaps it's the pressure we feel at work to deliver or the more acute pressure of that one-off crucial meeting when everybody is relying on you to make that important presentation and win the new business.

## Identifying your stress mindset will set you free

The idea of a stress mindset is fast becoming recognised as a concept. Studying individuals experiencing stress has never been more timely than now, amidst and in the aftermath of the COVID-19 crisis. On the one hand, there will be those who demonstrate resilience and find that the challenges posed by the crisis offer opportunities to sharpen their focus, give strength to their motivation and allow them to learn and achieve more. That is what is called a positive stress mindset. On the other hand, those people who see stress as something horrible and to be feared are demonstrating a negative stress mindset. People with a negative stress mindset will find stressful situations debilitating and this is where harm can be done as stress escalates and depression sets in.

## Resilience and tenacity

When somebody with a positive stress mindset is faced with a situation like this COVID-19 crisis, they will find the resilience and coping mechanisms to help them deal with it and find ways to work with the situation that will allow them to cope and to keep going. What allows us to show this resilience and tenacity is another product of our human nature, which might be hardwired into us or may have been acquired by our life experiences. Someone who approaches problems, obstacles and challenges with resilience can end up feeling energised by the fact they've made small but significant gains in the face of difficulties.

For someone who lacks the ability to be resilient or tenacious, the opposite is true. They will find themselves ground down by the stress of the situation. Studies by Alia Crum of Stanford University in the USA* show insight into how the positive stress mindset also affects adolescents. In the study, Crum and her team found that those young people who could see the potential benefits of a positive stress mindset ended up experiencing less stress when they were faced with challenging life situations. The findings of this study suggest that if adolescents adopt a positive stress mindset early, they will be more resilient to stress as they grow older.

## Turning around a negative stress mindset

Even if you are unable to be positive in the face of stress or you very definitely fall into the camp of the negative stress mindset, there will be ways in which you can turn things around. Crum conducted another study in which adults watched a film clip that concentrated on the possible enhancing properties of stress. After this, the participants were deliberately put into a socially stressful situation. The study found that those participants who watched the film reacted in a way that was more positive than participants who were shown a clip depicting stress as all bad.

One suggestion to help us deal with stress and help us develop more resilience and tenacity is, surprisingly, to go and watch a horror movie. This is because watching a horror movie and deliberately scaring ourselves can have a calming effect on the brain and will force our emotions to recalibrate. There is no doubt that most studies carried out will show that the more cheerful we are and the more resilience we can demonstrate, the better we will be able to deal with stress. For those who have a less optimistic personality, the reverse is true and their pessimistic way of looking at things and lack of resilience in the face of adversity will make them more stressed.

Now that we have explored how human nature dictates much of what we do, how we feel and how we approach things, we can get down to specifics.

Once upon a time, there was a woman, we will call her Shelly for now, who took a career break from a big retail bank. She had come to the point in her life where she was tired of the nine-to-five hustle and the unfulfillment that accompanied it. She needed some fresh challenges and so changed the direction of her career for what she thought was an attractive offer. It turned out to be a hoax because, although the new job materialised, the promised salary did not. So here she was, in limbo, until a friend, seeing the situation from the outside, told her that she really did not have a problem.

'What *is* the matter with you?' her friend said. 'The solution is right under your nose. You have all the qualifications you need, why don't you set up as a self-employed mortgage broker?' Shelly listened to her friend and considered her options, then she thought, what was there to lose?

In the next few weeks, she called up a serviced office company, paid a deposit and secured an office. She paid the first month's rent, then the second and then the third, but she had yet to put one foot inside the office. Why? The simple answer is that she was terrified, she was afraid of actually taking the plunge into self-employment, she was petrified of failing before she had even tried. Fear can be paralysing and Shelly was terrified of handling the Inland Revenue, scared of what the future had in store. It took a wake-up call for this woman to step out of the cocoon of fear and begin her business. A new year was beginning and she told herself that she needed to move and move fast to make up for the lost time she had suffered due to her fear.

'Shelly' was me over fifteen years ago, and that woman could also be you. After a faltering start, I took on my first client and I am extremely pleased that I took the step of faith and dived headfirst into running my own business. I do not belittle the fact that self-employment is hard work and can also be a lonely pathway, but it can also be very rewarding.

So, back to you, what has been holding you back? What are the things you are longing to do or achieve that fear or procrastination, even laziness, is holding you back from? Is it a mental block? Is it time for you to agree with me and begin to live your dream? It is so cliché but nonetheless true: every journey begins with a single step. No matter how long, treacherous or dangerous the journey ahead may be, you can only arrive at your destination if you take that first step towards it.

Who told you it is not possible? Have you attempted to start at all? Maybe family members and friends have told you it cannot be achieved? Are you sure that their actions don't come from a fear that they will envy your success if you make it? Maybe it is self-limiting beliefs. Well, to that I would say 'What proof have you got that you can't do it or make it work?

## Time to reflect

Write down the things you want to do that you have not started or achieved yet.

1. Write down what strengths and abilities you have that will help towards attaining your goals.
2. Write down the difference you will make with what you plan to do. Who needs your services? Who is going to be your audience?

3. Take a long, hard look at what category you think your idea falls into. Is this a talent or passion, a gift or a hobby?
4. If you could transform your idea into a full-time endeavour, would you be fulfilled?
5. Be honest and list the things that are stopping you from moving forward right now.
6. Be honest again and answer whether or not you could overcome your obstacles and how you would do that.
7. If you cannot go forward, why not? Who could help you to get ahead, and how different would you feel if you could have help?
8. Do you know anyone who has done something similar? If you do, pick their brains.
9. How would you feel if you died without doing what you have in mind? Is this your purpose or just a passing fancy?
10. How do you feel about leaving a legacy for others from what you have achieved?

These are just a few questions to ask yourself, the answers to which should show you whether or not you really mean business with the ideas you have. I am so passionate about purpose and I love the phrase of the great motivational speaker Les Brown: 'Live full and die empty.' These words mean so much to me as I truly believe in purpose and fulfilling destiny.

I also believe it is a good idea to read biographies and autobiographies. Read them and you will find that they are not only motivating and inspiring, they might also give you ideas. Hardly anyone makes it overnight and we all have to have a beginning.

I recently read the biography of Jo Malone, *My Story*, which tells of her journey from humble beginnings to the sale of her million-pound organisation to the Estée Lauder Corporation. When I am out and about and I see, hear or read stories about women like me, women like Jo Malone, I often remind myself of this funny thing – they do not have two heads. If they have achieved, then so can we, and I think we all have to do this from time to time, give ourselves a bit of tough love, get a bit of reality into our lives and stop messing about.

Looking in the mirror and taking a reality check can be really hard to do, but sometimes it has to be done. Nobody can speak to you like you speak to yourself. I still have those hard conversations with myself and I still have some goals I am striving for. I would urge you to do the same – stretch yourself to enable your dreams to become a reality. The greatest tragedy is when we leave things too late.

I recently coached a group of fifteen-year-old girls at a school in North London. I posed a question to them, asking where the greatest treasure in the world was buried. Some shouted 'Within us!', others shouted 'In our hearts', but one young woman piped up 'In the grave'. I was so shocked that she got it. I hugged her and told her she was absolutely right and it was true, too many people go through life not using their potential, talent and gifts and when they die it is too late – those gifts and greatness die with them. I am determined that this will not be my ending and I sincerely hope that you won't let that happen either.

If you are alive, you must dream, you must have something you are hoping for, something you are holding on to, something to look forward to. Surely this is what makes life interesting and breaks up the monotony of everyday living.

How would your life be if there was nothing to look forward to, no treats, no presents, holidays, celebrations, relationships, new homes, graduations, promotions, new births? How would you feel if your life was just bland and boring? Maybe it already is and if so, it does not have to be. Some people say life is what you make it and I agree – what you put in, you take out.

If you are alive, it is your God-given right to dream. Now is the time to stop making excuses and start taking up the challenges, it is time to make time for you! You are allowed to be self-centred when it comes to your destiny, the only reason to not be self-centred is if you have children. But it can be amazing if your children are able to achieve more than you ever did.

## Failure is not the end of the story

Action is everything, inaction is a killer – whatever holds you back, be it fear or personal problems, it may rob you of the chance to truly live and fulfil your destiny and purpose. Why would you deliberately miss out on what life has to offer you? You could be reading this book and saying to yourself, 'Lola does not understand my issues, she won't get that I have failed several times, she won't understand that I do not have the finances to get my start-up going. She won't understand my depression or my loss and pain. It's easy for her.' Ok, stop right there! Let me correct you.

I have been through loss, pain, depression, disappointment, tragedy, shame and a myriad of other issues and I know it's hard, but I have made a determined choice that I will not stay down! The day I discovered the importance of purpose and fulfilment is the day I decided that I would live my life to the fullest. It comes at a cost, but that is a price I have committed to pay.

Remember the boutique I told you I opened in the earlier chapter? Well, I did it but it failed, and when I failed I beat myself up. I felt ashamed – I did not take the failure well. I kept thinking about what people would say after all the fanfare of the shop launch and opening. It was a bitter blow to have to give up the lease and be left with a debt. It hurt so much that even just walking down that street after the shop closed I would feel sad. I kept the hurt deep within me, until one day, during a group coaching session, I shared my story. I spoke about how

I sourced the shop, how I had lovingly filled it with little bits and pieces from exotic places around the globe. I spoke of my customers, about the different types of people who would come in and purchase beautiful accessories from India, China and the UAE. I spoke about the clients from rich Arab nations who were regulars and the celebrity who purchased a pair of sandals (one of my favourite moments). Many of my clients commented about how my shop was like a home, it was lovingly furnished and although I had bought from popular stores such as Ikea, B&Q and Argos, I had styled it well. It was unique. It was me. I was proud of my achievement – and then things went wrong.

So, I was sharing my story within a narrative coaching session, and I realised the more I shared my story, the more the pain dissipated. The telling of my story became more and more therapeutic when I spoke about my failure and how I realised I needed to pick myself back up. I realised that in sharing this failure, the focus was on the event and *not* on me as a person. It was part of life's big experience and I had to put it behind me and move on to the next lesson. There is no doubt it was painful, it was very hard indeed and even more than that, it was disturbing. But now, hand on heart, I can say that I have been enriched because of the experience, and the failure of my boutique truly empowered me to use my talent as a coach and embark upon postgraduate coaching qualifications. It allowed me to give my full attention to my group coaching organisation.

What have you failed at? There may be several reasons why events did not work out as you had planned. Now, however, it is time to pick yourself up, dust yourself off, break through the cobwebs of rejection, self-pity and the fear of trying again and get on with whatever you wish to do.

Have you ever heard of the term failing forward? It means that failure can teach us some of life's greatest lessons. If you have failed, at least it was more or less confined to you and your immediate circle of family and friends. Think about those in the public eye who have experienced major failures in front of a smirking world. It must be really hard when everyone is aware of your failure and voicing their opinion on it.

The truth is that life is too short to constantly worry about what people are saying or thinking of you (they are still talking about Elvis Presley and he has been dead since 1977). The issue, whether their subject is dead or alive, is that people will talk, and you have to find a way to just not let it bother you. Who has never failed before, let him cast the first stone. In fact, failure comes only when you refuse to get up and dust yourself off – remember, the previous attempts were just trial runs!

It is now time to say emphatically 'YES! I will give it a shot.' It is very easy to hide behind the words 'it is not possible'; it is much more difficult to break free from a negative mindset than it is to embrace a positive one.

Fear, and the fear of failure, is a very powerful emotion; most of us, at some time in our lives, have experienced that fear and a loss of confidence. The physical and physiological onslaught of fear can be paralysing, sometimes leading to anxiety, panic attacks, depression and further manifesting in states like paranoia and claustrophobia, addictions, insomnia, weight gain or loss, physical pain, etc. Fear is a potent force, and not to be taken lightly.

Conquering fear is the greatest antidote to overcome this sometimes debilitating condition. These are some of the ways I deal with my fears:

First of all, recognise there is an issue and give your fear a name.

- Acknowledge what is causing you to feel fear.
- Try and distract yourself if possible. I work on myself via cognitive behavioural coaching so that I do not become too fixated on my fear.
- Challenge the fearful thought. Try and box it into a corner of your imagination by distracting yourself with something else and refusing to give it the limelight it wants.

- Engage in positive thoughts and imaginings. Think of a good outcome rather than a negative one.
- Share your fears with someone else. Their perspective might give you some very valuable insight (plus it is good to talk).

The mind is a very powerful piece of equipment. To be a success, you must decide whether your mind will control you or if you are going to control your mind. Who exactly is in charge? I sign off my emails with the words, 'Think it, See It, Live it'. These six words are the core of my belief system 'as a man thinketh so he is'. The greatness of any idea, or indeed anything we want to achieve, starts with a thought. This thought becomes visual in the mind's eye until it becomes a reality.

By the sheer will of human nature, you will keep pressing on, despite failures and disappointments, until the goal is achieved. You must get to a point where your mind and physical body are in perfect agreement and harmony and making the sweet music of achievement together.

## Do not let procrastination win

This leads me to talk about the enemies we must learn to free ourselves from, and we start with that old enemy that loves inaction: **Procrastination.** It has delayed and derailed the plans of legions of people of every creed, race, ethnicity, age and gender. It truly is an enemy of mankind.

What is it exactly? The dictionary describes procrastination as the 'act of putting off or delaying, especially something which requires immediate attention'.

I once attended a workshop where procrastination was explained further as putting off things you do not wish to do due to fear (which may be true in the case of some). However, you must recognise that it is a problem that affects many and if you are to get to the next level of your life, you must learn how to deal with this form of distraction. You need to get up and do something beneficial for your life, even when the sofa is so tempting and you feel safe there. We have all been there – just fifteen minutes more becomes an hour, then a day, a week, a month, a year and then a decade. It is so scary what inaction can do.

It scares me that time is the one thing that man cannot control. We have been to the moon and explored space, made all types of advances in technology, engineering, science and medicine. But we have not been able to do a single thing about time. The more time we spend on planet Earth, the less time we have left. Procrastination is a bona fide robber of time. 'I'll do it tomorrow,' you tell yourself. The fact of the matter is that tomorrow may never come – where do you think the old adage 'make hay while the sun shines' came from?

## Laziness does not lead to success

Another enemy of humanity is laziness. This is described as the inability to use energy or work, or as downright idleness. A motivational speaker whom I very much admire, says that we should work hard now so we can rest later. As the mother of a young student, I had many a conversation with my son about laying off the PlayStation and studying hard so he could also make his own financial choices, just like the owners of Sony PlayStation were doing today because of their earlier dedication.

Success without hard work is near impossible – there cannot be any glory without a well-weathered story. Laziness, however, robs man of the ability to explore opportunities. It robs man of ideas and potential and it hides gifts and talents in the quagmire of idleness.

PLEASE NOTE (HENCE THE CAPS), I AM NOT TALKING ABOUT AN OCCASIONAL BOUT OF LAZINESS. I AM TALKING ABOUT WHEN LAZINESS BECOMES A LIFESTYLE.

I think it is important for us to take time out and do nothing from time to time because we all need time to refresh, recharge, renew and refocus. I am writing about those who eat the bread of idleness. Those who do not try to better themselves, those who cannot be bothered to do anything and likely become a liability to those around them.

Laziness can be extremely debilitating. It can prevent a life from being fulfilled and prevent accomplishment even where there are skills and talents. The following may help to overcome any form of laziness:

- Take time to focus on what you need to achieve (this may involve you taking a weekend away if applicable to really get it clear in your mind).
- Remove yourself from any distractions so that you have the chance to really concentrate.
- Break down your assignment into smaller chunks that do not seem so overwhelming.
- Get an accountability partner (this could be a mentor or a coach to keep you on track, someone you respect who will give you the kick in the pants you need, when you need it).
- Make an effort and decide a date when you are going to put your plans into action. Then stick to it!
- Set an alarm or a default diary for the task so that you have a map of what you are going to do, and when.
- Constantly check in with your accountability partner.
- Reward yourself for continued progress, saving a big reward (something you really will love)for the end of the task.

Laziness does not have to win, you can win this, you do not have to allow laziness to keep you on the sofa of no direction. The truth is that we are all products of the choices that we make. Decide that you can do this and get it done. May I also add that laziness may be a quick route to poverty. The sofa is not going anywhere, but you sure can.

To be successful sometimes requires sheer determination, hard work, dedication to the cause, commitment and dedication to the purpose. Pounds will need to be saved in the bank of consistency, resilience, hard work and diligence.

## Do not get distracted from your end goal

Finally in this chapter, I would like to focus on another key ingredient in the 'make it but do not bake it' cake, and that is the very horrible-tasting distraction.

Distraction can rear its ugly head in just about every facet of life. We need to be especially resilient to deal with and overcome it. But what is it? In simple terms it is when life gets in the way, preventing you from focusing on the task at hand. It can be a diversion, a disturbance and, if we are really harsh, we can call it a nuisance, especially when what we are distracted from is very important.

How can we overcome it? Well, we need an extra helping of resilience and the magical words, 'Focus! Focus! Focus!'

Just as something as powerful and soul-destroying as bereavement can throw us off balance, so can breakdowns in relationships, depression, births, stress and the influence of television and the media. Life issues get in the way of simply *doing life*. The key to overcoming distraction is to empower your mindset.

Hold on to your dream, goal and purpose. Be determined that it is too important to allow distraction to gain control. Many people state that there are not enough hours in the day and to overcome distraction, you are going to have to adopt a very disciplined mindset. You may almost have to adopt military precision, accounting for every hour, minute and second. I find that a default diary works well for me. Time management is everything and you will find that if you plan your schedule in advance and try your hardest to follow through, you will leave less room for distractions.

The steps to overcome laziness may also be applied to counter-attack the time-wasting strategy of distraction.

Oh, by the way, just in case you did not know, John Logie Baird invented the first television and is also noted by the BBC as one of the '100 greatest Britons'. He definitely made his mark, although the television set, like my Mac Ruby Woo red lipstick, can also be called a weapon of mass distraction. We can sometimes waste so many man/woman hours worshipping at its altar: news, reality, documentaries, soaps – the list goes on. Please do not misunderstand me, I am not condemning the television, I am simply stating that we must get the balance right. If we are determined to rid ourselves of procrastination, laziness, distraction and other vices, we may be on the journey to winning.

## Time to reflect

1. What do you need to declutter – is it a thing or a mindset? Nail it down.
2. What is bugging you or distracting you; what would you like to be free of?
3. On a scale of 1–10, how motivated are you to declutter your mind and to focus on your future?

## Tip

Procrastination is the thief of destiny!

# CHAPTER SIX
## *DRESS TO IMPRESS*

There is a statement which I love and I think it is so very true: 'You dress the way you wish to be addressed.' As humans, we *do* judge a book by its cover, even when we are told we shouldn't. It is human nature and it is so easy to jump to conclusions and form an opinion about someone based upon their appearance or mannerisms.

A very interesting article in *Psychology Today* written by Leonard Mlodinow is entitled 'How We Are Judged by Our Appearance'. In it, he says that we all know that looks matter. What most of us don't understand is just *how much* looks matter – and how difficult it is for us to ignore a person's appearance when making a social judgement.

Mlodinow goes on to say that he is talking about all our human interactions, not just the romantic ones. He also says that his observations are not just to do with perceived 'beauty', but also with the very many other qualities of our appearance.

In everything that we perceive, from how we see things to what we gauge from our hearing to how we understand someone's character, when our unconscious mind starts its assessment it will make that assessment according to the data available, helping us arrive at a fuller picture based on what that conception has been. It will help us to construct and shape the complete picture.

To arrive at this complete picture, our unconscious mind will employ educated guessing and some clever tricks to help it fill in the blanks. When we assess people and when they assess us, the subliminal mind will take the limited data that it is given and create a picture that seems right and is probable. It arrives at these conclusions from things that are inferred unconsciously and gleaned from aspects such as the other person's body language, their appearance, how they are dressed, their voice and what appears to be their social category.

Politics is an area in which the face has been studied a lot for social cues. And there is no time when this scrutiny is more apparent than at election time. Mlodinow tells of the importance of visual cues on voters when they were assessing who they could trust in office, and with their vote. This is a decision we make all the time when we make a judgement on things like who to date, to hire and to trust. When it comes to making this kind of judgement in a political candidate, Mlodinow wanted to find out how accurate we would be in making a judgement about whom we should trust.

Mlodinow found out that a candidate's appearance, their look of competence can trigger a change in voting patterns. The effect, he found, was not only powerful but it was also subliminal.

Mlodinow mentions one study by political scientist Shawn W. Rosenberg of the University of California, Irvine, where 140 volunteers were recruited and told they would participate in a study about voting in which they would be assessing candidates hoping to be elected to Congress in three districts nearby. The volunteers were shown two fliers that had information about the candidates and that included party affiliations and their opinions on different issues. There was also a photo of each of the candidates.

In actual fact, all the information had been made up for the experiment. The men in the photos were models dressed in a suit and tie and in a prior survey with a group of different volunteers, they had been marked high or low for qualities like leadership, competence and integrity.

The researchers arranged for half the people in the survey to see the candidate with the best appearance and were told that he was a liberal Democrat, while the rest of the survey members were told he was a conservative Republican. This should mean that regardless of the politics of the survey participants, the two men in the photos received equal numbers of votes, provided that their looks were not a factor. In fact, what happened was that the more handsome candidate led the vote at about 60-40.

So, it is clear that we are influenced by what we see. After all, when we first meet someone, that is all we have to go on, isn't it? It always amuses me when people say that you are 'shallow' if you discount someone, especially in a romantic way, because of their appearance, when they could be a lovely person underneath. We are visual creatures and if we don't like the packaging, we are not likely to want to find out what a person is like underneath. That is the truth of it. It's like choosing a meal; you are going to go with what appeals visually (remember the old saying – you eat with your eyes).

There will be people who say, 'what is the big deal about dressing up, what is so important about your appearance?' Stay with me as I tell you a story.

A few years ago, I attended a speakers' conference in London. The host of the conference, a well-known speaker in the industry, was hosting a training event. He began with an introduction to one of his top protégés. He spoke very highly of this woman, how great she was and how she was a leading light in the speaking industry. I should say here that the speaking circuit is still mainly male-dominated, so I was excited to see her and hear what she had to say – and then she appeared. I was so disappointed and because of this, I could barely concentrate on a word she said. The reason? Her dress was way too tight and her stomach was bulging against the fabric. It looked awful, and no, she was not pregnant! Her appearance was distracting and I asked myself, how could she leave her house dressed like that, let alone stand up in the middle of a room full of people? My opinion of her was that she just looked sloppy and I couldn't take her seriously. Harsh as this may seem, that was my reaction. I believe that as women, more so than men, our appearance matters, and I am not talking about our size. It is about putting it all together, making the best of ourselves, and that is possible at any weight or height. Every woman should have a full-length mirror, and if you try something on and find that it is too tight, then wear something else, or wear some control garments. The moral of this story, for me, is that the way you are dressed can distract but not always in a good way.

A few years ago, I attended a personal styling course at the London College of Fashion. I came away with some valuable nuggets, some of which I will share with you. The first is that most people look better with clothes on rather than off (surprise, surprise). Secondly, sometimes it is best to buy a size bigger rather if it fits better and, lastly, it seems that red is a colour that gets a woman noticed by the opposite sex.

Your appearance is your 'shop window' for who you are, but dressing to impress does not mean you need to dress expensively or in high-end designer gear from head to toe. My interpretation of dressing well is to know your body and to be comfortable with your shape and to dress accordingly. Then dress to your body's strengths and very importantly, to your personality. Dressing to impress does not mean you need to be a slave to fashion, chasing after the latest fashion fads – it truly is about embracing you, warts and all. As women, our shape is often labelled as being apple, pear, plum or banana. The jury is still out for me on this analogy; I am not sure if we should be comparing our body shapes to pieces of fruit in the first place – after all, how many pieces of fruit have you seen in a Tu outfit? However, what is key is that different styles suit different body shapes.

I have a curvy figure with well-pronounced hips and I love pencil skirts because they really suit me. A woman with endless legs may look great if she is wearing a thigh-skimming dress. Tiny waists, full busts, curvy bottoms, beautiful shoulders, etc. all have particular styles that show them off best, whether that is nipped in at the waist, halter-neck, mini, etc.

Without sounding patronising, what may let a lot of women down is the inability to be totally truthful and accept their body shape. This may prevent them from accentuating their strong features. Every woman has something fabulous about her – it could be her eyes, her hair, legs, breasts, hands, feet, personality, etc. Don't you think it is time to celebrate your best features and show them off? Who knows, this may also help to boost your confidence.

It is also important to accept the things that you cannot change. A while ago, I remember that I was trying on a pair of dainty shoes. They did not fit and in frustration, I said, 'What is the point of wide feet, what purpose do they serve?' There was a sudden silence and I heard a small voice say, 'And what if you had no feet?' I shut up immediately and have not complained since. I have accepted my wide size-eight feet and the knowledge that dainty shoes and sandals are not for me. I just have to be content to admire those styles on others.

Without a doubt, it will take time to totally accept what you may deem as your flaws, but our quirks and imperfections are what make us human. I often say that even the most famous supermodels probably have a feature they wish they could change. In 2015, there was an online article by *Cosmopolitan* magazine that covered a range of models and their body insecurities. Some told the story that when they were younger, they were called 'giraffes' because of their height. Imagine the stick that

Cindy Crawford would have got for the mole on her face, which now is her defining feature and simply adds to her uniqueness!

Approximately a year ago, I was running one of my Proudtobeme self-esteem workshops with a group of fifteen-year-old girls. To my surprise, every one of them, without exception, stated that if they could afford it they would consider plastic surgery. This totally threw me and I was sad to realise how much pressure women, both young and old, heap upon themselves simply by measuring themselves with someone else's yardstick.

Women are doing so well in the big wide world, but there is still a long way to go in the area of low self-esteem. The media does not help with their portrayal of perfection and photo-shopped celebrities in every magazine and on our screens day and night.

This takes me back to over twenty-five years ago, to when I visited the United States of America for the very first time. All the ideas that I had of black America were rooted entirely what I had seen in *Ebony* magazine. Wow, I was in for a shock! The reality was such a let-down to my naïve self. The glamorous women I had seen on the magazine cover turned out to be decidedly ordinary. This was my very first introduction to the power of photoshopping, good lighting and glamorous settings, which are not real life.

I cannot stress enough how important it is to develop your own unique style and embrace your individuality. What size you are really should not matter. However, if you are particularly bothered about your weight then there is always something you can do about it. As much as we are in an age of political correctness, if you take two women and put them in the same dress, one in a size 12 and the other in a size 28, for example, let's be honest, who will look better? We could argue this until the cows come home, but the fact remains that if you asked one hundred people, most would choose the woman in the size 12 as the dress would fit and fall better. It would look right and proportional to our eye. That is not to say that if you are bigger there is no way you can look good. You can – again, it is a matter of finding out what suits you and what you feel good in.

In my opinion, there should be a few staples in your wardrobe, dependent on your body shape and your individual preference:

- A flattering jacket or blazer, maybe in black or navy blue
- A pencil skirt and an A-line skirt
- A couple of well-fitting shirts or blouses in colours that complement your skin tone
- A pair of trousers (style dependent on body shape) in a neutral colour
- A shift dress
- A fitted bolero, a cardigan (I sometimes wear one to cover up my arms)
- A pair of jeans in a flattering cut
- Accessories, accessories, accessories (jewellery, bags, scarves, hats, gloves). Some like to keep it simple – a string of pearls and a simple pair of earrings – and some like it bold and brash – it is totally up to you! Accessories can jazz up an outfit and also help you put your unique stamp on it. My go-to accessories at the moment include really large necklaces and lots of brooches.

I often tell people that if you are travelling, you have more chance of an upgrade if you look the part. Last year, my eyelash technician was off on her holidays to Dubai. I explained my golden rule to her and she passed this on to her travelling companion, and they both dressed smartly. On her return, she told me that although she did not get a flight upgrade she did get an upgrade on her hotel room. It works, maybe not all the time, but it did on that occasion.

The fact is that first impressions really do count and you hardly ever get a second chance to make a first impression. I once attended a personal branding workshop where the speaker informed us that, on average, it takes forty-four subsequent meetings to cancel a negative first impression. Is it likely that you will get the opportunity for forty-four other meetings? Not really. So, the motto of the story is that you must make that first meeting count. It is better to be unforgettable for the right reasons. We live in a very visual world and people who are eloquent in speech, appearance and manners, and who are confident in themselves, will generally get themselves noticed.

Personal grooming is important and it speaks volumes about who you are. You may agree or not, but as we have seen from the study earlier in this chapter, it really does make a difference.

As a serving magistrate, I see many defendants in the dock and there generally seem to be two approaches to making an appearance in court. The first type of defendant will turn up in joggers and a hoodie, or jeans and a tee-shirt, while the second type will appear in a suit or similarly smart attire. Although justice is dispensed regardless of whether the defendant is in joggers or a suit, the impression given by attire could mean that the defendant considers the proceedings to be really important and that a good impression needs to be made, or that they think the proceedings are unimportant and they cannot be bothered to dress up. The same mentality applies to interviews – most people will dress smartly for an interview, simply because they want to make a good impression, bringing us back to the adage, 'Dress the way you wish to be addressed'.

If, for example, you were going to meet your bank manager to ask for a start-up loan, what would you wear? Would you dress to impress, as a businesswoman who takes her work seriously, or would you dress as though you were off shopping?

It is a hypothetical question and the choice would be yours, of course. Without stating the obvious, turning up in smart business wear will definitely win you some brownie points and make your bank manager more confident that he was authorising a loan to someone who took their business seriously. Tempted to wear a low-cut top and a Wonderbra? The bank manager may be a woman, but even if it is a man, he might not appreciate the insinuation that his decision could be swayed by your 'assets'. The way you appear can be a key selling point, and you should use this to your advantage.

When I did my personal styling course, I vividly remember one of the students who was also on the course. I was surprised at her appearance. As a stylist in training, her clothes were shabby and un-ironed and the tracks of her weave were on show and half hanging off. Her appearance shocked me and I initially thought that possibly it was a financial issue. But speaking to her, I realised that this was not the case. I could not think why she would choose to present herself that way. I am not too sure of the type of clientele she thought she would attract because it is often said that you buy from who you like. If there is something about you that your clientele finds attractive, the more likely it is that they will imagine themselves working with you. Personally, I would not seek styling advice from someone who looked as though they needed to do some serious work on themselves!

Colour is a very important element in your style wardrobe. You may have a natural affinity for the colours that suit your skin tone, or you may feel comfortable in a simple black outfit. In the winter months, however, when we all tend to stick to browns, greys and blacks, it can be nice to jazz up the darker colours with bright accessories.

I cannot stress enough how important it is that how you dress will speak volumes – you may not think others will notice but I can assure you that they definitely will! In the celebrity world, when they get it wrong, we have all seen how disastrous and embarrassing the consequences can be. Who would want to feature on the worst-dressed list? No matter how thick-skinned they may be, the jokes and subsequent discussions about their appearance cannot fail to undermine them as artists and it would be hard for them not to lose focus.

Away from the world of celebrity and stars and back to the world of mere mortals, it is also important to have a regular wardrobe detox. If you have not worn it in six months to a year, maybe it is time to sling it out. Maybe you still love a particular item and it is now either too small or too big? You could take it for tailoring amendments, and that would have two advantages. The first is that you will save money by not having to buy something else and the second is that you also get to keep a favourite outfit!

Here are my Top 9 tips for achieving a positive first impression:

- **Tip one** – every woman should have a full-length mirror at home so that she can see herself from all angles.
- **Tip two** – if you do not feel comfortable in an outfit, follow the adage 'If in doubt, leave it out!' I remember I was once in a shop changing room and I heard the shop assistant telling a customer that she looked fabulous. The truth was she did not and I could see that the shop assistant was just keen on making a sale. As women, we will know instinctively what looks good or not and our comfort level is a strong indicator. We must always be brutally honest with ourselves and have the strength and dignity to leave well alone if an outfit is not totally right for us.
- **Tip three** – do not let delusion dress you up. It really is not a good idea to try to squeeze into that size 10 dress when you are now a size 16! No one knows you like you do and even the best stylist should not be allowed to get you into an outfit that you are totally uncomfortable in.

- **Tip four** – do not allow yourself the temptation to become a slave to fashion. Remember that fashion is fickle, so be your own best friend and develop your own unique style and know that not all styles suit everyone. Wearing what suits your body shape and personality and that compliments your uniqueness will be far more rewarding and will boost your self-confidence.
- **Tip five** – ooze confidence. This works best if you are not inappropriately dressed As much as we dress (whether we admit it or not) for others, try and please yourself first – you know what suits you best, after all. When you are happy and confident in how you look, you walk with your head high and your shoulders straight, and heads will be turning for all the right reasons. When a woman's self-esteem is low, it reflects in her gait. She might almost walk as if she wished she would disappear, with her shoulders hunched and head bowed.
- **Tip six** – celebrate your best features and show them off. If you have not discovered them yet, then please make every effort to do that. Listen to what other people say, the compliments that they pay you, and you will normally get a good idea. Once you know your own USP (unique selling point), accentuate those attributes, do not hide them away – you owe it to yourself!
- **Tip seven** – as much as you celebrate your best features, at the other end of the spectrum, you need to learn to live with the things that are less than perfect. Plastic surgery is a really drastic option and it also comes with risks and no guarantee of results. There are some things, like my wide feet, that I have just accepted, and I believe this is my best option. My wide feet are not like breasts which can be adjusted upwards or outwards with the wonders of surgery – I have simply accepted my lot. I wear shoes which fit my feet and avoid any that make my ankles look

too large or my feet stubby. I now tend to wear shoes and boots which lengthen my calves.

- **Tip eight** – mix and match your wardrobe. If you have a unique look, then trawl independent boutiques, they can be a treasure trove! I love to look different and I have found some great bargain buys and some unique pieces online in independent stores and they were not necessarily that expensive. A while ago, celebrity chef Nigella Lawson wore a dress from a certain boutique in Central London for her court appearance. The boutique's website crashed and I laughed to myself. Why? Simply because not everyone would look like Nigella in their dress. We can sometimes be quite gullible when it comes to fashion, forgetting that height, shape, posture etc all make a distinct difference to how we look in an outfit. Reflect back on who-wore-it-best images and you will understand what I am talking about.
- **Tip nine** – simply be you! No controversy, there is only one you, so be you and live you with no apologies.

## Question time

1. How would you describe your style?
2. If money were no object, would you buy more expensive pieces?
3. Are you confident about the way you look?
4. Are you a slave to fashion or do you have your own quirky style?
5. Are you comfortable with your body shape? If not, how motivated are you to work on it?

## Tip

You dress the way you should be addressed!

# CHAPTER SEVEN
## NETWORK, NETWORK, NETWORK

*'As iron sharpens iron, so a man sharpens the countenance of his friend.'*

**- Proverbs 27:17**

One of my favourite phrases, which I also find the most meaningful, is 'No man is an island' and this is so true. Who on this planet can claim they have reached their destination by themselves? As long as we are members of the human race, we need other humans to assist us on our journey of life. The most successful and the richest people in the world have all relied on others to help them climb up corporate and financial ladder. It is people that make the world go around, and networking is vital for that. We often hear about multimillion-pound deals being done on the golf course or in the club or some other place where like-minded individuals gather.

Another truth, particularly in the world of employment, is that it is those individuals who make a point of going to the pub with the team/bosses who tend to get promoted. What this means is that people make people and we are all pieces in the jigsaw puzzle that is life – we just need to find the part that we fit in that jigsaw.

Away from the world of business and career and in the treacherous world of dating and meeting new people, how will we ever meet new people if we never get out there? Maybe you like to date online – well that's fine, but you will still need to go out and physically meet people! Networking is so vital in today's world, but with the rise of technology, it can be easy to be insular. The advent of COVID-19 has definitely not helped in that respect and when we can, meeting up for a coffee is still as vital as it has ever been.

I have met some of my closest female friends at networking events and we have enjoyed many years of female bonding and fellowship. A key strength of the majority of women is that we truly want to empower each other and we are pretty good at connecting with each other and connecting each other to other people whom we believe may be useful.

Networking can be a cost-effective tool to expand your range of contacts. But networking must be approached with common sense and diligence. I am not a fan of paying thousands of pounds to join a networking organisation as I do not believe that they offer true value for money. With this in mind, it is important to choose carefully who you network with so that you can ensure you are not paying over the odds for the privilege.

From my personal experience, it may be best to attend a networking event alone because if you attend with a friend or colleague, you may be tempted to stick to each other throughout the event. If you attend alone, you will mingle a lot more easily. I would also recommend that you wear something that will get you complimented so that people come over and tell you that they like your shoes, necklace, dress, etc. This will break the ice and get the conversation flowing.

I would also advise swallowing your pride or shyness and being determined to make conversation, even if you are rebuffed at first. However, since everyone is there to network, you should find people as eager to mingle as you are.

It is also important to be careful about how you phrase your opening questions. I do not like the question, 'So, what do you do?' because, for me, it sometimes sounds more like 'What can you do for me?' If you approach networking from the perspective of 'how can I be of service?', that will always be best.

Networking should be fun and fresh, not boring and stuffy. Try not to take yourself too seriously and try to separate the wheat from the chaff of attendees. Hard-nosed, pushy people are not hard to miss as by their fruits you shall know them, and there are definitely some bad apples out there.

It is also important to appear confident, state your name clearly and move around the room – do not get stuck with just one other person. To get the most out of networking you need to meet everyone. Do not spend all your time speaking about yourself and your achievements – in this sort of setting, it will always pay to spend more time listening than speaking. However, prepare an elevator pitch beforehand so that you can outline what you do succinctly. Make mental notes and try to remember names. It is so important to be polite. Aim to communicate without using profanity or suggestive remarks. Try your best to be friendly and leave what may be going on in your personal life at the front door.

The most profitable networking events I have attended have had nothing to do with financial profits, but I have started some great working relationships from them, which have opened some fabulous doors in my career advancement. It is important to remember that post-networking is important and to follow up with specific attendees, not simply add them to your mailing list.

It is a good idea to give your business card only to those with whom you truly wish to keep in touch. Ensure you send a timely follow-up email, possibly within two days, along the lines of 'It was great to meet you, I was truly impressed with your work and I would love to meet up over a coffee.' Humans like to have their egos stroked and as long as you are genuine with your compliments, you will get their attention.

Networking events or similar are great places to find a coach or a mentor. A few years ago I heard that Richard Branson had five or six mentors. I took a long, hard look at myself and told myself that if this was truly the case, then I would need at least one! A mentor or coach is invaluable in the world of work or business because you do not have all the answers. We should all take a drink from the well of valuable experience. I often joke that experience is not sold in the supermarket. There is great power in effective collaboration and as women, we sometimes do this particularly well.

**Networking in the right way can be a very low-cost and effective marketing tool.**

Through networking, you have the opportunity to increase your visibility, your sales and your contact base through introductions and referrals. This could either be at face-to-face gatherings and meetings or maybe, since the days of restricted movement due to the coronavirus pandemic, you could also network through email, on the phone, through business networking websites, on Skype or Zoom. However you choose to go about your networking, make sure that it works best for you. As with everything about networking, it needs to be tailored to you and your business. It is definitely not a case of one size fits all.

Although you should concentrate on the people directly related to your area of work, it is always worth keeping in mind as you go, that there may be other helpful networking contacts who might be outside your sphere of work, such as lecturers, counsellors, scientists and other educators, for instance. Make sure that when you are expanding your networking reach, you keep in mind people who, while seemingly not directly relevant now, may have something to add later on.

Let's look at putting together an introduction speech or as it's also called, an elevator pitch. Think of it this way. You meet somebody in the lift that you've been trying to get to see for ages. You are travelling up six floors together. She asks you what line of business you are in, and you have only the time until the lift doors open again to tell her and to make an impression. That is just how long your elevator pitch should be, so there is no room for waffle. Boil it all down to a few well-chosen, impactful statements.

There are five primary things that you will need to adopt if you are going to be successful in business networking.

**Make sure your elevator pitch is concise and to the point, but do not stint on bigging yourself up either.**

1. **A good elevator pitch**

   - The first thing you need to get over is your name. Extend your hand, smile and make eye contact so that you appear confident, even if you're feeling a little shy or nervous. Keep your attention on the person you are speaking to. There is nothing worse than someone constantly looking over your shoulder because it implies they are waiting for someone better or more useful to come along.
   - Next, you need to say who you work for or what your business is. You can follow that information up with the question 'Maybe you've heard of us?' If the answer is yes, then add more, perhaps updating them on a recent development. If the answer is no, then you have an opportunity to fill them in on some more details about your company.
   - You should also add where you are based and what area you cover. This provides the person you are speaking to with some context and helps them to imagine how you might work together.

- Practise all of this before you go to your networking event and try your best to stick to it. Somebody who is rambling and jumping from topic to topic randomly will come over as unprepared.
- You should aim to finish your pitch within twenty to twenty-five seconds. Remember, you won't be the only person at the networking event and the person you are speaking to will appreciate not being bombarded with too much information when you initially introduce yourself.
- The best networkers know it is always good to end with a question rather than let the conversation just die out. You should also make sure you understand a bit about body language so that you can detect if somebody is really not interested in what you have to say and is itching to move on to somebody else who may be more relevant to them. Asking a question about the person you are meeting or about their interests or history in a company shows that you're interested in something other than your own concerns.

2. **Don't blend into the crowd. Be individual and make sure you stand out for the right reasons.**

   **Standing out from the crowd**

   - It can be a crowded marketplace out there and you need to somehow develop your own Unique Selling Proposition (USP) so that you stand out from the crowd. If you were a hairdresser, for instance, you could offer a service at home as well as in the salon, or specialise in wedding or special occasion updos. Anything that differentiates you from the norm will help people remember you.
   - Take a careful look at how you describe yourself and your offering and make sure it is going to catch the eye of potential customers by showing your flair and individuality, either on your business

card or through any other method of advertising. You really need to think outside the box for this one. If you are struggling to find a difference between you and other people, consult a publicist or a brand expert.

- Make sure that your USP is watertight so that if you are asked questions, you are convincing in your answers. Have a look at what your competitors are doing and aim to improve on that.
- Always be positive. Use positive body language and affirming language. This will get you noticed and draw people to you.

3. **Make sure you offer help to other people where you can and you will find yourself on the receiving end of reciprocal assistance.**

**Help others – give before you receive**

- You should always make a priority of helping other people before you take for yourself. I am a strong believer that you have first to give so that you can receive. A good phrase to remember is 'What goes around comes around' – karma is always there waiting to pay you back or trip you up, depending on how you have behaved towards other people. Being helpful and kind to other people will always get you good results. People will remember your kindness and they will reciprocate in the same manner. This type of behaviour will earn you a good reputation for being someone trustworthy and in my experience, once you have established that trust in people, referrals follow.
- Make sure the words 'What can I do for you?' and 'Can I help you?' are always on your lips. If you are at a networking event and see somebody who looks new and a little lost, be the person who takes them under their wing and introduces them to others.

4. **Make sure that you are honest in all your dealings. Always show yourself to have the highest integrity. People need to know they can trust you.**

   **Always keep your integrity**

   - Without integrity there can be no trust, so this is an area that you need to be really careful with. Think carefully about the decisions you make because you can easily damage your integrity beyond repair.
   - As humans, we all make mistakes. If you do slip up and make a mistake, then make sure you own up to it and apologise immediately to ensure maximum damage limitation.
   - If you are determined to grow your business, then your reputation must grow alongside it so that people come to know they can trust your word, and that you are somebody who always backs up what they say with honest action.
   - Always follow up on things that you have promised. If you say you are going to call someone, call them; if you arrange a meeting, then make sure you are on time – nothing annoys people more than having to wait for someone to show up.
   - While you will want to be known for being reliable and dependable, you need to ensure that this is not taken advantage of. Have your own boundaries and gently but firmly enforce them. People will soon learn that although you are reliable and dependable, you are not just there for them to dump on at any time that suits them.

5. **Avoid a scattergun approach to networking and target only those people and organisations that are most relevant.**

   **Seek relevant groups and connections**

There are several things to keep in mind when you are trying to make good connections for your business. These can be relevant to you in terms of:

- the size of a business
- the sector it works in
- demographic grouping
- geography
- associated trade group
- any other common interest,

The more specifically you target prospective contacts, the better the result will be. You will waste your time and effort if you wander aimlessly from place to place, chasing every contact without prequalifying their suitability for what you can offer and what you would like from them.

Most people who are successful have a small group of trusted associates beside them; at the early stages of setting up your business, it is great to have these people, but it is also important to choose them wisely.

Here is an example of how you can make your own networking planner.

| | |
|---|---|
| What is my goal? | |
| Who are my ideal connections? | |
| Names of some groups | |
| What is my elevator speech for this group going to be? | |
| What can I offer the people I am approaching? | |
| What would I like these people to offer me? | |
| Provisional dates/related tasks | |
| My outcome aims | |
| Actual results | |
| Amount of time spent on the task | |
| Compare with my other marketing activities | |

## Ask yourself these questions:

1. How can you increase your confidence to network?
2. Can you make a list of relevant networking organisations that you can attend?
3. What will you do to develop confidence in the art of networking?

## Tip

Make sure that, above all else, you always show that you have integrity and are serious about your business aims.

# CHAPTER EIGHT
## EXCELLENCE IS KEY

*'Whatever your hands find to do, do it with all your might, for there is no work, or device or knowledge or wisdom in Sheol (the place of the dead), where you are going.'*

**- Ecclesiastes 9:10**

A couple of years ago, I spoke at a sixth-form college in East London and somehow we got into a conversation about Harrods, the world-famous department store. We discussed how Harrods made us feel and we all bonded, students, staff and facilitator, over one word and feeling that Harrods evoked in all of us, and that word was 'special'.

The thing is that, as soon as you walk through the doors of Harrods, you are transported into a world of luxury, excellence and the exciting possibilities of dreams fulfilled. There is something very special as Harrods invokes a feeling that is very different from any other luxury department store; I could describe it as being an almost magical feeling that anything is possible. No wonder then that Harrods' mission statement includes the following:

'To be the number one department store in the world for luxury branded merchandise, maintaining an unprecedented level of retail standards expertise.'

From the staff to the branding, Harrods oozes luxury and puts the customer first, and although this very probably costs millions to achieve, they make it look effortless. And that, I believe, is the secret – it is important that, no matter how small your business, you always aspire to excellence, even if you are a one-man band. Excellence gets you noticed; it truly makes a difference. No one remembers the mediocre, and the terrible is remembered for the wrong reasons. Excellence is always remembered, as people tell their friends how delighted they were with the service they received.

If you review all the iconic global brands such as Apple, Amazon, Google and Coca-Cola, at their hearts, lies the customer experience. That might be at the level of understanding their customer base/target audience, moving with innovation, embracing their passion for the product, which has a knock-on effect on the target audience, and offering consistency and competitiveness of delivery and product. Add in great marketing and influential leadership and you have the seven top characteristics of successful brands, according to an article by Forbes.com.

As a mentor of young women, I sometimes organise afternoon teas and lunches at iconic venues such as Harrods and The Dorchester. The reason I choose these venues is to inspire and empower young women in the area of choice and aspiration. My coaching and mentoring organisation empowers young women to 'Aspire, Achieve and Acquire'.

The Dorchester offers outstanding service and you can feel the spirit of excellence from the moment you walk through the door. Whatever you are doing right now, excellence is what you need. The top hotels and restaurants on the Trip Advisor website have earned a certificate of excellence because they have strived to be above average and give the customer a very good experience.

I have been blessed to have been able to travel to most continents on Earth. Each travel journey is unique, the staff, facilities, food etc. all make a huge difference to your perception and enjoyment. However, some trips have remained unforgettable to me just because of the excellent service I received. (Other trips have been unforgettable for totally the wrong reasons!)

I would take excellence any day. Why excellence, you may ask? Because it gets you noticed, and the same philosophy can be applied to all you do – in your career, in business, with your hobbies, your studies, in fact, anything that you do.

Before I plunged myself into the world of self-employment, I worked for a high street bank, working my way up from a cashier. Even then, I had a strong work ethic motivated by diligence and excellence. I know that not everyone loves their job, but it helps if you do because you wake up each morning with a spring in your step. It is no secret that many employers will be more partial to employees who meet deadlines, who are passionate about their work, are punctual, who keep absence to a minimum, who are diligent and, when needed, are team players.

Employees who are really good at their job are invaluable. It also helps if they have a good attitude, which may include a dose of humility. I understand and am aware that we are all different in our approach to work, but it really does help if you are simply nice to people. Anyway, back to excellence!

We are all familiar with life in the twenty-first century as we try to juggle work commitments, our families and our own self-improvement. We all want to be the best version of ourselves that we can be, and we all want our businesses and ventures to be successful. But we also want our families and ourselves to be successful, happy and healthy. Those things are great and they make for a great springboard to what I think is the most important thing to strive for, and that is excellence in everything.

At this time, with countries, economies and homes ravaged by COVID-19, it may feel like a big ask to be striving for excellence when it is a tough enough job to survive from day to day. But humanity will rise and we need to be firing on all cylinders to make the most of any and every opportunity that comes our way.

I know that you would like to make your mark in the world and that you believe in what you're doing, and in the product or service that you are offering. If you can live a life of excellence, there is no doubt that you will leave your mark on this planet and also help other people along the way, so here are 20 ways in which you can achieve excellence in your life.

1. **Know your values**

   In order to make the right choices in your life, you have to know what your core values are. Make sure that you know and stick to those values. Although there will be some values that stay with you throughout your life, you may find yourself adding others to the list along the way, so revisit your list often.

2. **Don't be afraid to stand up for what you believe in**

   Most of us will have an opinion on something, and if you feel strongly about anything, you should never be afraid to speak up for it. This will give people an impression of you that will label you as somebody of firm beliefs who is not afraid to stand up for what they believe in. Do not be afraid to express your opinion or even to take action when you feel strongly enough about a cause and feel that it is worth fighting for, whether that is an environmental issue or an issue of human rights. Your voice and your actions can help.

3. **Be a good listener**

   You can learn an awful lot by listening to people, and people definitely love being listened to, especially those who have been where you are trying to go and whose experience will be invaluable. When you are a good listener, people see you as an excellent person to confide in and trust.

4. **Be in touch with your emotions**

   When you are really busy with work or trying to build your business, it can be difficult to stay in touch with your emotions as you try to keep a business-like attitude. To really achieve excellence in what you are trying to do, you need to stay in touch with your emotions, acknowledge them and work with them.

5. **Be cyclical**

   Just as life and our planet move in circles and cycles, so you need to adopt this type of ebb and flow in order to remain flexible and achieve excellence. Sometimes the way ahead of you may be blocked. If it is, then go around it, under it, over it – go any way you can, but always head for the top. Use your flexibility to pursue your excellence.

6. **Be mindful and meditate**

   I have mentioned it before, but meditation and a mindfulness approach to life can be powerful tools when you are striving for excellence. Having a quiet, meditational approach can show you solutions that would never otherwise occur to you in the frantic business of everyday life.

7. **Keep a journal**

   This is very useful to everyone, especially those pursuing excellence. Record everything, from your thoughts about life and your ideas for your business to books you need to read or references you want to look up – write it down and refer to it later. These are the building blocks of excellence. Keeping a record and being able to look back and evaluate things that you have thought about or done in the past can be invaluable in helping you improve on the excellence that you are aiming for.

8. **Identify the things that are holding you back**

   Take a long, hard look at what is stopping you from achieving the excellence you are craving. Are you afraid of failure? Do you think the mountain is too big to climb? Do you lack confidence in yourself to see yourself through? Do you think your background or your gender is going to limit your opportunity? Really identify the things that are holding you back and then address them one by one. At the end of your examination, you will find that there are not as many fears lurking to trip you up as you thought there would be.

9. **Be thankful**

   Becoming complacent is the biggest threat to achieving excellence. However small, always be grateful for the positive things that make the journey easier. Start each day by writing down ten things in your life that you are grateful for. Even in your darkest hour, there will be things that you treasure and that you can feel gratitude for, like your family or your good health.

10. **Be cheerful**

    To achieve excellence you need to be seen as someone confident and content. That means facing the day with a smile on your face to show people that you are in control of your life and that you are on top of everything. Even if things are not going that well, smile and you will feel the benefits. Remember that old saying, 'misery loves company'? Make sure that you are never the companion of misery and that you ensure your excellence by approaching each day with a positive attitude and a cheerful demeanour.

**11. Be compassionate**

Nobody who has achieved excellence is jealous and bitter. There is no doubt that on your way to the top, there will be many people trying to trip you up, but judging them and being bitter about what they have done is not going to help you on your journey. Instead, try to imagine things from their point of view and show compassion for them. We all have bad days and we all say things we wished we had not. Do not be quick to judge but do be quick to show understanding.

**12. Study your dreams**

This may sound a little bit strange, and I know that a lot of the time we do not remember what we dream, but if you do have a dream and remember it, then write it down and have a look at any online site or a dream book to learn more about the message that your dream has sent you. Your subconscious will hold all kinds of messages for you and it is your job to interpret them.

**13. Be a teacher**

On your way to excellence, you can help others who are coming along behind you. Use any unique gifts that you have to pass on information and guidance to others. Give talks or set up a workshop. Your generosity of spirit will repay you and you may also find the missing piece to your own jigsaw amongst the people you meet.

**14. Address the past**

All of us will have things in our past that we are less than proud of. Perhaps it is the way we treated somebody that has always niggled us. In these cases, you need to cut out the cancer and address the instance that is eating away at you. Try to put things right so that you can continue on your journey to excellence with nothing holding you back.

**15. Challenge yourself**

Nobody ever achieved excellence by taking the path of least resistance. To truly make yourself, your business or your service the best, you will have to constantly challenge yourself. A coach or mentor would be great to help you do this but if you do try and fail, don't beat yourself up, simply learn from your mistake and do better next time.

**16. Rejoice in your body**

No matter what size or shape your body is, whatever you like or don't like about it, always treat it well. Your body is going to be with you for life and you need it to stay the course. That means nourishing it well and taking the time to exercise. Indulge it with a bit of luxury as well, like having a massage or an occasional candle-lit bubble bath.

**17. Use your brain**

You will doubtless have heard it said that we only use a small part of our brain. Make it your business to push your brain as far as it can go as you strive for excellence. Do crosswords or enter into lively debates so that your brain gets the same exercise as your body. Keep your brain open to suggestions and to learning anything new that you can pick up along your journey.

**18. Be forgiving**

As important as forgiving yourself is for anything that you do wrong, you also need to forgive others for their transgressions. Excellence was never achieved against a background of resentment and festering anger. Let it go and free yourself for the more important journey that you are on.

**19. Put your focus on being rather than acquiring**

We are all driven to some extent by the consumer society and it can be difficult to resist those messages about the tech that we really have to have. Partly, this is because we need tech and a lot of other things in the world around us. But more important than this is focusing on yourself and who you are, and judging yourself by this measure rather than the material things that you have.

**20. Have you done your best every day?**

At the end of every day, ask yourself if you really have done your very best on that day. Have you helped yourself towards your goal of excellence and helped other people along the way too? Learn to identify the things that motivate you and cultivate them.

According to the Office for National Statistics (ONS), the UK currently has about 4.6 million self-employed people. Many of these will be running small businesses and according to Small Business UK, after five years of trading, just four in ten small businesses will still be trading. There are various reasons why small businesses fail, with the number one reason being a lack of cash flow. However, I believe that your small business has a better chance of survival if you follow this advice:

- Research your product and subject matter. Sometimes, in a start-up business, we are told that the best thing is to look for a niche. That is always a good idea, but after attending various workshops, I now realise that such opportunities do not appear up and down every high street. What will make the difference and allow you to stay in business is a demand for what you sell. However, it is important to research your product and look at the numbers. A business plan is key, especially if you think you will need to borrow money from the bank. There is a debate as to whether a business plan is really necessary for a start-up and to some extent I believe this is a personal choice. The thing about a business plan, however, is that having one will allow you to plan, review and execute your ideas.

- Getting a thorough knowledge of the product is always essential. One thing that you can do, for example, is a short course on your subject matter. I did that before I opened my boutique. I signed up for several courses at the London College of Fashion, and I have to say that those courses were invaluable and saved me a lot of money when I started the business.
- If you can, do a bookkeeping course or, if you feel it is easier, get someone to work for you on an occasional basis to help you with your finances. If you are not good with numbers, this will prove invaluable.
- If you are employing staff or an assistant, especially as a small company, it is important that you hire someone you know you can work with. The world of self-employment is notoriously lonely, so it is important not to add strained and fraught relationships to the mix.
- On the topic of hiring, it may be a good idea to hire undergraduates or new graduates who are looking for experience on an intern, volunteering or a part-time basis. From my own experience, I love working with young people because the majority of them are teachable, coachable, and they will often have really fresh ideas. You may also find them useful in the areas of website set-up, social media and more specific fields such as online marketing. However, never try to get people to work on the cheap. Resentment is not a good motivator and you need to pay people properly to get the best out of them and to feel good about yourself.
- It will be a great help to find a mentor within your business. There is no substitute for experience and if you can sit at the feet

and learn from someone who has walked your journey previously, it really will be a great help. There are many entrepreneurial organisations that will offer free mentorship in your chosen field, whatever that is. It is important, however, that you find the right fit for you, and that will include a synergy in personality and character type. Organisations that offer free mentorship include:

- Mentorsme.co.uk
- Micromentor.org
- Womentoringproject.co.uk
- Startups.co.uk
- The Institute of Enterprise and Entrepreneurs.

There are many more, so I suggest that you discover what organisation works best for your business.

- Many people are unclear about the difference between a coach and a mentor. As a postgraduate qualified coach, I can assure you that they are distinctly different and this is how you know the difference: A mentor will show you and a coach will push you. A good coach will push you beyond what you think you can do so that you can achieve the goals and objectives you might have thought were impossible. A coach may also serve as an accountability partner and/or a critical friend. There is usually a cost, although some work pro bono. Finding the right fit and chemistry is key. A major difference between the coach and mentor is that the coach does not necessarily need to have experience in your sector.
- This is simple but so needed – try your best to approach your business with total honesty for the best chance of seeing it succeed. You cannot afford to approach your handiwork from a position of mediocrity. Extraordinary and excellent people/products truly get noticed. This may require you to think outside of

your comfort zone. It may also require you to be more sociable, to up your creative streak and to generally up your game. You can do this if you take a long, hard look at your business, through genuinely self-reflective eyes. Sometimes only you can speak the truth to you and truly get through.

- Rome was not built in a day, as the saying goes, and there is no doubt about it – you will have to be resilient, consistent, patient, hardworking and a hundred and one other things that will have to be unearthed on your journey to your destination – the top! Indeed, failure does not define you. Take any successful entrepreneur and check out their past. I am sure that failure would have appeared in one chapter of their lives, even if it was only fleetingly. I am someone who has failed in the past and, as painful as it was, I have learnt some empowering lessons from the journey and I can share them with you now, without feeling ashamed. Failure does not define you – true failure comes only when you decide not to get back in the saddle. The spirit of excellence empowers you to keep going until you succeed.

The mindset required to succeed in the battle that is life is an all-encompassing one. You may wonder why I describe life as a battle, and the answer is simple: in my opinion, it sometimes is! It truly is a matter of survival of the fittest. You must take your place and fight to win the prize of a satisfying and fulfilled life. This will come when you have an abundance of fulfilment in all spheres of life. True prosperity may include good health and well-being, peace of mind, financial strength and abundant hope for a brighter future. At this point, I must also add that another phase of prosperity is the ability to give back. A life that adds value to the environment and community is truly a blessing to others.

As we have seen, excellence encompasses many components and a good starting point is to review and reflect on the way you have been approaching life in the past. Maybe there is a course you need to attend or even complete. It could be that you need to engage with a coach or mentor. You may also need to review your product or service with a view to expansion, upping your game, being bolder or more creative. You need to do all that you can to be outstanding in whatever you do. Excellence begins with you. You must make it a way of life, embrace it, feed it, live it and evaluate it daily within your life.

Excellence is also cost-effective as it is a way of life and it can distinguish you and your brand, give you great results and set your product or service apart as above the ordinary.

## Ask yourself what you could do to give your product the edge.

1. What do you think a mentor could do for you?
2. How could a business coach help you improve your offering?
3. Where do you see your business in five years?

## Tip

Always remember this helpful hint – feel the fear and do it anyway!

# CHAPTER NINE
## GO FOR IT

Maybe you are sitting reading this book and however old or young you are, there are still things you wish to achieve. As a mature woman (yes, I know some people hate that word!) – well OK, as an older woman – I know that you cannot please everyone. However, I am of the older demographic and I must admit there are still some things I wish I could do. Firstly, I wish I could play a musical instrument, a guitar to be exact. I always wished I could play because I can sing and it would have been so wonderful to be able to play along with my singing.

My son has inherited my musical streak and we were having a discussion on all things music during which I mentioned how much I regretted not learning to play the guitar. My dear son almost told me off and said, 'Mum, it has nothing to do with age – if you want to learn, just get on and learn!' And he was right; for too long I had been curtailing myself, boxing myself into a corner because I felt that I was too old.

My mentality and view of life have now totally changed. Age is a number, it is not a barrier. It should not be constraining and it is definitely not defining. Ageing just means that you have less time to spend on the planet, so what do you need to do? You need to LIVE. Live life, treat each day as if you are running for the last bus that will take you to the place of your dreams. I have embraced this standpoint.

I remember a conversation I had with my partner. At home one day, I was busy complaining about how busy I was and how my diary was jammed full. My husband looked at me and laughed and said something I will never forget and which had a significant impact on my life. The magical words were, 'The trouble is, you are only running on 40 per cent capacity of what you truly can achieve.'

Wow, that was profound! From that point onwards, I decided to truly up the pace of my life and run after the last bus as if my life depended upon it. I threw off the shackles of constraint and decided to truly live, and although I did not take up the guitar, I did decide to do other things that would make a real impact.

Chase your dreams! Live your dreams! Let me tell you, you are never too old to live out your dreams. It is all about how badly you want them! The dream you had at 18 can still come true even when you are 60, it's all about how badly you want it.

Chase your dream and do not stop until you catch up with it and pocket it. There may be many reasons you think that you cannot do it. Maybe the barrier is funds, but I can tell you from personal experience that if you really want something badly enough, there is every possibility that you can achieve that dream.

I am a firm believer that your past should not determine your future. Maybe things have not gone according to plan. However, millions of others face the same obstacles; what is going to make the difference is how you deal with it. It is important to move on, drop the heavy baggage you are dragging around with you and reach out and grab your destiny with both hands. Regret and despair make very bad bedfellows and we have to make a conscious decision to leave them behind us and move on. A life full of regret will be a barrier to fulfilment. The future is a new beginning and has so much to offer.

It is important to challenge yourself, to stretch yourself to go where you never believed that you could get to. This may involve change. It is great being comfortable, however, no one ever became unique, historic or left a famous legacy just by being ordinary. Extraordinary people get noticed and applauded but mediocrity is rarely rewarded. Stepping outside your comfort zone requires courage and determination, but if you have the nerve to take those steps, the rewards can be great. Take a step and do not be intimidated by failure. It is a great learning curve and, although you may not appreciate it at the time, you are bound to learn from the experience.

## See the best in yourself

Review your life from a positive perspective – if you do not believe in yourself and your ability, how on earth can you convince anyone else to believe in you? You have to see the best in yourself; this is not always easy, however, you must learn to overcome limiting beliefs and self-doubt and trust in yourself, and be confident that you have something positive to offer to planet Earth. It is my firm belief that all of us in the human race were born with gifts and talents, some more than others, sure, however, every one of us has something to offer to humanity. It may be time for you to reflect on your gifts, potential and talents and hone them where you need to.

## Drop negative people

The book of Proverbs states that 'As iron sharpens iron, so one person sharpens another'.

I have heard it said in networking circles, that your network determines your net worth. You may not agree with this statement, but it is true that if you surround yourself with the wrong people, they may have a negative effect on your life. Likewise, surrounding yourself with ambitious and confident people could exert influence in a positive way. The key is who is in your network – are they supportive and encouraging? Do they believe in your ability, or are they dream killers and dream stealers? Do they tell you that you can do it, or do they say you will never make it?

A while ago, I decided I would only keep people in my life who would contribute to my life positively and therefore add value. I do not have the space or time for the excess baggage of negativity. My friends and acquaintances are mostly high-achievers who are also eager to give back and to make a difference, as clichéd as that may sound. The desire to add value to others is a key pointer in my relationships and I simply dislike those whose lives are preoccupied and consumed with only themselves. Surrounding yourself with the right people is so vital in today's competitive world; after all, no man can break through without a leg up from a friend, colleague, family member, etc. Of course, there has to be some form of give and take, so having an attitude that makes people want to assist you is also essential.

One thing that will help you improve your game more than anything else is to play against somebody better at it than you are, whether that is in tennis, poker or any other game. Whatever it is, if your opponent is better than you, it will help you raise your game. You will have to think faster and work harder, but that will help you improve faster than you would have done without the competition. You will certainly sweat and your muscles will ache, but pretty soon you will find that your skills have improved and eventually you should become good enough to teach somebody else in the way that you were taught. And this analogy does not only apply to sports; it applies to your career and your personal life as well, and that is why it is important to choose your friends well and always surround yourself with successful people.

I remember somebody once telling me that they had been to a symposium and for three days they listened to people who were top entrepreneurs and entertainers and true leaders in their fields of endeavour. Of course, my friend was inspired by listening to the words of some truly amazing and inspirational people, and by the time the symposium was over, she was feeling full of inspiration, had all types of new and innovative ideas and felt truly empowered by what she had heard. This is the effect that exposing yourself to influence from people who are better than you can have.

These are some practical steps you can take to ensure that you have only the best around you in your own life.

## Do not entertain negative nellies

Nothing brings you down faster than people who are permanently negative and who second-guess everything that you say or plan to do by tutting and shaking their head and saying, 'Do you *really* think you should do that?' And then there's the other type of influence in your life, the one that comes from the person who is in a continual cycle of drama and always seems to be in some sort of pickle or another. Hang around with them for too long and you find yourself in a race to the bottom with them.

There is no doubt that life is difficult enough and we know that we can't always win, that there will be challenges along the way. Some things cannot be helped and we just have to find ways to deal with them as they occur, but we can choose our friends and influencers wisely so that we are influenced only by the positive and never by the negative. Remember, you want to surround yourself with people who are going to make you up your game rather than bring you down to their level. When you float a tentative idea that has an element of risk, you need to have people around you who say that they know you can do it and that you must take the chance, *not* that it is a hopeless idea and you'd be crazy to try it.

Nurture relationships with people who elevate you and get behind them as well so that you can have a mutual admiration society that will make both of you the best you can be. As I have already said, life is far too short for negativity to be allowed in.

## Always hang out with people who are cleverer than you

A lot of business people and entrepreneurs are constantly vying to be the cleverest person in the room and the authority on every topic that is raised. But here is the thing, if you are always the cleverest person, you are actually placing limits on yourself. In fact, it is very common for us not to appreciate the importance of the people we mix with.

As I have said, we need people around us who are going to push us and challenge us to be better. That starts with teachers and, if we are lucky, includes the influence of people in our families and trusted friends as well as possibly, later on, mentors and coaches that we might employ to help us achieve our dreams. Also, if we are focused on how clever we are, we may miss the opportunity to see what other people are doing and aspiring to, which we might also achieve if only we had the humility to observe. When we have the right circle of influencers, the bar will always be raised and we will always have higher expectations of ourselves than we had before their influence was exerted. Sometimes we will embark on a course of action or a plan simply because we have seen other people succeed, and in that way, we will improve ourselves. Having positive people around us will always be a game-changer and help us to be the best that we can be.

## Have relationships with people who have already walked in your shoes and achieved what you want to achieve

With more and more people relying on social media for their communication, we can easily lose sight of the importance of the real-life relationships that we have. Social media can be a very useful platform, but it can also be a very negative influence, with trolling accounting for a lot of misery and even death amongst people who have been hounded to suicide from its negative influence. The kind of person who feels insecure and undervalued is not the kind of person you need commenting on your situation or your accomplishments on social media. Their jealousy or resentment will skew their view of what you have or will achieve. Highly successful people are usually also willing to share information with those aspiring to their success and will also be the kind of people who make things happen. They will be people who have learnt from the mistakes that they have made along the way and will be an invaluable source of tips and tricks that will help you avoid similar pitfalls. That is why you should always make every effort to find people who are leaders in the field you want to succeed in and pick their brains for any information they might have for you.

With that in mind, have a good look at your contacts both on and off social media and decide which ones are really supporting you and which, given half a chance, would like to see you fall flat on your face.

## Watch what is going on and be observant

Even when you are less than expert in something, there is nothing to stop you from observing other people working at it and learning from what they do. Avoid ever becoming so arrogant that you think you cannot learn anything, and make sure that you have your eyes open so that whatever happens around you, you can soak it up like a sponge and adapt it to fit whatever you are involved with.

## Empower your well-being for the journey

According to Statista.com, the health and wellness industry in the UK is worth over €25 billion, and some of my money is contained in that figure, no matter how minute a portion! Keeping an eye on our health and well-being is really important and ideally, we should avail ourselves of every opportunity that comes within our reach. This might include attending the gym, fitness classes, engaging in healthy eating and partaking in regular exercise of your choice. It is also important to maintain a healthy mind and it is so heartening to see that the issue of mental health is now becoming more and more of a mainstream topic, especially with high-profile people speaking about their personal battles with issues such as depression and anxiety.

I once had a conversation with a GP friend about mental health and she explained it so succinctly when she said that she often tells her patients that if they had a broken leg, they would not ignore the pain and injury and that they would not hesitate to seek help. Her point was that if they had a problem with their mental health, they should approach it in the same way as they would a physical problem.

There should be no shame if you ever think that you need to see a therapist, psychologist or psychiatrist for any issues you may be facing. Your emotional, mental and physical well-being is paramount if you are going to stand any chance of reaching your potential.

## Time to reflect

1. What do you think is holding you back from reaching your potential?
2. What steps could you take to make it easier for you to reach your potential?
3. Who would be of most help to you in achieving this?
4. When are you going to start changing things?

## Tip

Think it, See it, Live it!

# CHAPTER TEN
## *WOMEN LIKE YOU*

Recently I was reading a very important piece of information from the UN about the empowerment of women.

## Facts and Figures: Economic Empowerment

https://www.unwomen.org/en/what-we-do/economic-empowerment/facts-and-figures

**Benefits of economic empowerment**

- **Women's economic empowerment is central to realising women's rights and gender equality.** Women's economic empowerment includes women's ability to participate equally in existing markets; their access to and control over productive resources, access to decent work, control over their own time, lives and bodies; and increased voice, agency and meaningful participation in economic decision-making at all levels from the household to international institutions.
- **Empowering women in the economy and closing gender gaps in the world of work are key to achieving the 2030 Agenda for Sustainable Development** and achieving the Sustainable

Development Goals, particularly Goal 5, to achieve gender equality, and Goal 8, to promote full and productive employment and decent work for all; also Goal 1 on ending poverty, Goal 2 on food security, Goal 3 on ensuring health and Goal 10 on reducing inequalities.

- **When more women work, economies grow.** Women's economic empowerment boosts productivity, increases economic diversification and income equality in addition to other positive development outcomes. For example, increasing the female employment rates in OECD countries to match that of Sweden, could boost GDP by over USD 6 trillion, recognising, however, that growth does not automatically lead to a reduction in gender-based inequality. Conversely, it is estimated that gender gaps cost the economy some 15 per cent of GDP.
- **Increasing women's and girls' educational attainment contributes to women's economic empowerment and more inclusive economic growth.** Education, upskilling and re-skilling over the life course – especially to keep pace with rapid technological and digital transformations affecting jobs – are critical for women's and girls' health and well-being, as well as their income-generation opportunities and participation in the formal labour market. Increased educational attainment accounts for about 50 per cent of the economic growth in OECD countries over the past 50 years. But, for the majority of women, significant gains in education have not translated into better labour market outcomes.
- **Women's economic equality is good for business.** Companies greatly benefit from increasing employment and leadership opportunities for women, which is shown to increase organisational effectiveness and growth. It is estimated that companies with three or more women in senior management functions score higher in all dimensions of organisational performance.

In this chapter, I have decided to hone in on the saying that iron sharpens iron. We all have a story that needs to be told, whether we are famous or not, and over the years, I have interviewed some women who, although they might be considered ordinary, are doing great things and I am delighted to share some of their journeys with you.

## Lydia's Story

I realised that how we each interpret success can be different and so I interviewed a few women who have established various types of businesses and asked them all the following questions:

- What is your definition of success?
- What were your dreams as a child?
- Who has been the biggest influence on your life and what lessons did you learn?

First was Lydia, an award-winning entrepreneur. She created a natural skincare brand and the 'keep it immaculate' face mask.

Lydia's definition of success is whatever she decides is successful – she sets no limits.

Lydia describes herself as being successful when everything she wants comes to fruition; she is constantly creating success within her goals. Her advice when it comes to challenges is that you should not remember the things that have gone wrong; once they have been dealt with, she says, just move on. This resonates with me as I know that we can get stuck in a cycle of fear and failure.

In answer to the question 'What would you do if this was your last day on earth?', Lydia replied that she would spend it with loved ones and catch up with things that she had not previously done. Lydia added that her last day would definitely be spent with people rather than on anything that was business-related. She told me that the most important people in her life were her parents and the people within her inner circle and her greatest influence has been her mother, followed closely by Oprah Winfrey.

Why Oprah? Lydia chose Oprah because she had developed herself and conquered her inner self, including a very successful journey spent highlighting people, relationships and the highly competitive world of broadcasting media.

Lydia felt that the most important lesson she had to share was paying attention to yourself and she gave the example that we should listen to our intuition, listen to our inner selves.

Life is about creating memories and when I asked Lydia to tell me about one of her most poignant memories, she spoke about taking her stepsons to the country that she grew up in, the beautiful nation of St Lucia, and in this context, I do not use the word beautiful lightly. St Lucia is an absolutely serene and stunning place; if you can, please put it on your holiday bucket list. But back to Lydia. She enjoyed sharing her culture with her boys and it made her reminisce about her great-grandma, who waited patiently for Lydia and her siblings to come back to the island on a visit from the UK. Once they did and she saw their precious faces one last time, Lydia's grandma looked up to the heavens and quietly passed away.

Lydia also shared a memory of declaring at a networking event that she would become an editor in a year and how she went on to achieve it.

I asked Lydia if, on her life's journey, she had ever felt like giving up. She answered me with an emphatic no. 'It never feels right to quit but it's okay to change direction and alter strategy, and be honest enough to admit when it is not working.'

We spoke about community work and giving back and Lydia told me that she served as a McKenzie Friend at tribunals. The website https://www.mckenzie-friend.org.uk gives this description:

## McKenzie Friends - What are they?

If you cannot resolve your legal dispute through mediation, it may be necessary to make an application to the court to have a situation resolved or, alternative(ly), you may have become a defendant or respondent in legal proceedings.

Often you may find yourself being taken to court by your ex-partner and may have little choice. It can be extremely expensive to engage a solicitor to help you and Legal Aid is only available in special cases. If you elect to become a Litigant in Person, you will need to be able to present your own case to the court and this can be a daunting task both before, during and afterwards.

A **McKenzie Friend** can best be described as anyone who accompanies you to court to help you as a Litigant in Person - those who are unrepresented by a solicitor or [do not] engage a barrister. Your McKenzie Friend is able to sit with you in the court and offer advice and support as well as taking notes to help you.

There are some things that a McKenzie Friend cannot do on your behalf, such as conduct litigation, file court documents and statements etc. There is a Practice Direction issued by the Family Courts which explains this in more detail.

Our team of McKenzie Friends support[s] children and their families to help resolve family conflict. They are experienced, with many having successfully represented themselves in a court as a Litigant in Person. Others are professionally trained - some are qualified as a paralegal and others with a law degree or other professional qualification.

When we spoke of tough decisions, Lydia told me about the choice she made about giving up her office and deciding instead to work from home. In her office, she had garnered a reputation as a big sister figure and leaving the office meant that all the staff would have to go their separate ways; it felt, she said, that she was in effect breaking up the 'family' unit'.

The next step for Lydia included diversifying her business and embarking on a training school. There was no doubt that I felt inspired by speaking to Lydia, a woman with the determination and the drive to make her life a success.

www.keepitimmaculate.com

## Mo's story.

Mo is a single mum, a business owner, chartered accountant, a university lecturer, motivational speaker, author, professional networker, a mentor and a trainer. Her personal definition of success is achieving her goals and exceeding her targets. Mo hates being stagnant as she believes that is the same as going backwards. Mo told me that she was very proud of the success of her children. She is also extremely proud to have earned a first-class honours degree in Mechanical Engineering and be a homeowner on the way to achieving more of her goals, all by herself.

When I asked Mo to look back on her childhood, she told me that she remembered reading *Reader's Digest* at the age of seven and through that, developing a love for adventure. She also remembered accompanying her father to the office and finding, to her surprise, that he had a boss! It was a seminal moment for Mo and she knew from an early age that she would never be an employee.

Mo told me that her greatest challenge had been finding herself at one point living in a hostel, young, alone, scared and vulnerable. If today was her last day on earth, Mo said she would take the opportunity to tell people that she loved them, make peace with all those who she may have offended and, if she had more than a day left, she said she would travel.

When I asked Mo about the most important people in her life, she spoke about her children. As a single mum, she had given up quite a lot for them.

Mo's biggest influence was her father. She told me that she admired her father immensely because, as far as she knew, he had never taken a day off work and at the ripe old age of 77, he still went into the office every day, despite having had two knee replacement surgeries. Her father, she told me, had endured many tragedies, including the loss of more than one child.

Another major influence in Mo's life was her late grandmother, who was born in the early1900s and passed away in 1994. Although born in Africa in an age when women had limited rights, her grandmother was determined to leave a legacy for her daughters. She succeeded in that and by the time she passed away, each of her daughters had their own home, provided by the income she earned selling kola nuts. Mo's grandmother decided to be a strong, independent woman with access to her own money. She taught Mo to be strong, resilient and powerful. She lived by the motto 'Never give up'.

When I asked Mo about the important lessons she has learnt from the journey of life, she spoke about always reaching for more and staying on the path of resilience with dogged persistence.

We have all had moments when life has put us through the mill. When asked if she had ever wanted to give up on her dreams, Mo was quiet for a moment and then told me about the time when she was in the middle of her professional accounting exams. At that time, she had a young child and was overwhelmed with the demands of motherhood and study, coupled with the fact that she was also a single mother and so was doing it all on her own.

When Mo's daughter was born, she attended revision classes, took some time out to study and when her results came in, although she was expecting failure or a referral, she had passed! She remembered one of her study mates, who had no children but had not passed the exams. With two children, Mo passed first time. Mo recalls that this was her season of persistence. She studied hard, invested her spare money in books and immersed herself in study methods, mind mapping, note-taking and research methodology.

If Mo had another shot at life, she told me that she would have started her career earlier and maybe focused on media and marketing, and she hopes she would have written more books, including fiction.

In her spare time, Mo is a volunteer for the Women's Institute in Barking and Dagenham, and she is also very interested in film production.

## Dr B, GWIIN

As I interviewed Dr B of GWIIN, I asked her for her definition of success. She replied that to her, success meant a number of things, including happiness, contentment and having some material things. Dr B explained that she had gone through various stages of success at different times. She told me that she wanted to look back and see that she has achieved her various goals.

And her dreams? Dr B told me that, growing up, her childhood was not a happy one; in her words, it was 'emotional turmoil' – her parents divorced and amidst child custody battles that were very acrimonious, the young Dr B decided that she would never get married, although part of her yearned for a happy family life.

The greatest challenge for Dr B has been overcoming financial obstacles and starting her business with zero funds. However, whatever the adversity, her tenacity in business has had a huge impact and she has held events in all parts of the globe. The budget has been overwhelming many times and often seemed unachievable, but Dr B has always managed to overcome her challenges.

And what if today was her last day on earth? Well, Dr B told me that she would pray to God for forgiveness and pray for all those she would be leaving behind, then she would be prepared to meet her maker.

When I asked about the most important person in her life, Dr B explained that there had been different people who have been important at various stages and times of her life. I can truly identify with this; in fact, I am a staunch believer that we all have different seasons in which different people will appear in different capacities.

The biggest influence in Dr B's life has been her mother, who has taught her many lessons, the most important being tenacity, followed by persistence and the will to survive. Her mother was an amazing role model who put her children first and pushed them to succeed.

If Dr B could teach the world a lesson in a moment, it would be to have greater tolerance, to love more and leave the world a better place than you found it.

Dr B's happiest moments were having her children and once, during a visit to the nation of Iceland for a GWIIN event, when it turned out that the president's wife could not make the event as her father had been taken ill, so the president represented his wife.

When asked if she had ever felt like giving up, Dr B replied that she had, several times, but she always stops herself from thinking that way and finds reasons why she should keep going.

She believes that it is okay to feel you want to give up, but she thinks that your faith must keep you pushing on.

In the area of volunteering, Dr B gives her time on several boards and each month she identifies someone she can help in the community.

When I asked about the toughest decision she had made, she explained that this involved leaving her family to establish her consultancy company overseas, in the Middle East. If she had the opportunity to start another business, she would concentrate on an organisation that focused on social impact. In her own words, 'it is important to give back to the community and support other women.'

## Time to reflect

1. What would you like your legacy to be?
2. Who has influenced you, and how?
3. What will your influence be?

## Tip

Always keep your eyes on the horizon, move around obstacles, over or under them, but always keep going!

# CHAPTER ELEVEN
## *MY STORY AND A HIGHER POWER*

As I write these words, I am going through one of the toughest periods of my life and it is no exaggeration to say that the only thing keeping me going is my faith. Many people, at this point in time, all over the world, are in lockdown, and although it is not a nice feeling to be stuck indoors, I have a lot of other matters on my mind.

As I write this book in April 2020, it is a very strange time to be on planet Earth. The COVID-19 pandemic has wreaked havoc, with thousands of deaths worldwide. We are advised to stay at home and only go out if necessary, and with this in the background, I am also going through a personal issue that is eating me up and causing me so much worry. If it was not for God, I might go crazy.

When the lockdown began, I told myself that since I had a lot of time on my hands, I needed to bring out my laptop and finish the final two chapters of this book. I admit, I had worshipped at the feet of procrastination for way too long; I had allowed business to get in the way. I had not been practising what I had been preaching. However, I have repented of my sin and got myself back on track – and here we are.

I would like to go back and share with you a little of my background; I think that it's important for you to know where I am coming from and how I have arrived at my current destination.

I was born in London in the 1960s to immigrant parents who came from West Africa at a time when immigrants were faced with stark public notices. Wherever they went they read 'No blacks, no dogs, no Irish.'

I grew up in Penge, South East London, and I have many fond memories of school holidays spent in Crystal Palace and Anerley Park with my friends.

My younger years were quite uneventful, until, that is, my father decided that he was going to return to West Africa to settle down and my mother, my four siblings and I were to follow him. This marked the turning point, and I can still remember when my father (a dapper dresser) left for Africa in his pigskin jacket. That was the last time I would ever see him hale and hearty.

Within a few months of his returning to Africa, he had a stroke and the world as I knew it was turned upside down. My family went from being fairly comfortable to facing extreme poverty, with my father sick in Africa and the rest of us in London without a breadwinner. My mother had five children to take care of, all on a typist's small income.

I still remember the day that the electricity was cut off and how I knew, young as I was, that life had taken an unexpected turn, from good to much worse. Then, suddenly, my mum announced that we would all be going to live in Nigeria to be closer to my father, who had been paralysed by the effects of his stroke.

Fast forward to 1981, goodbye to my UK friends amidst tears, anguish and trepidation, and hello to Nigeria, another very unfamiliar world.

It was an enormous culture shock arriving in Lagos. Part of the problem was that we had been fed horrible stereotypes about Africa, prejudicing our minds, with the youngest of us even going as far as calling it 'the jungle'.

I have to admit it was tough, it was a shock and we faced poverty like I had never known or could have imagined before. It was a horrible experience, with the depth of our misery made complete by the death of my father in November 1984.

Being poor in Africa is a completely different world from being on the poverty line in the welfare state. The only saving grace is that, in Nigeria, you have friends and family who may support you, but there is a limit to how much you can ask of them.

We did have some support, but for the majority of the time, we faced real hardship. It was tough and remained that way for several years. I completed my first degree in Nigeria amidst poverty which was, at times, unbearable. I remember my 21$^{st}$ birthday. What should have been a day of celebration, was very painful. My mother did not even have the funds to buy me a card; we couldn't afford much and what money we did have did not extend to a greeting card.

Several years later, I graduated and completed my national youth service and my mum decided to return to the UK, hoping to lift us out of the poverty that had been our lives since my father died.

My mother did return to the UK and one by one, my four siblings joined her and picked up the life they had left off in South East London, in Clapham South to be exact.

I stayed in Nigeria because I had begun working in Lagos and was staying with a wonderful family who treated me like a daughter, and I am still close to them now.

After working in central Lagos for a while, I met my husband. We married and we had a son. But things were changing in Nigeria, and with the advent of a military government and the hardships that came with it, we decided it would be best if we relocated to the UK. I would return with our son and my husband would follow.

Life had gone full circle and I was back in the UK and in a flat in Haldane Place in Earlsfield, SW18.

After a while, I got a job with Halifax as a cashier. I got my own one-bed flat. My husband came to join us and I felt that life had truly begun!

We got a council flat in Battersea and my husband, despite his banking background, decided he wanted to go into full-time ministry.

I must admit that, growing up, I could be quite self-centred because my siblings and I had to literally struggle for everything. If you needed something or you needed to get anything, it was all about DIY (do it yourself). I took this into adulthood; however, as I got older and my attitude matured, I realised that life does not revolve around me and would be more enjoyable and beneficial if I added more value. This is one of the reasons why I love philanthropists such as Bill Gates and others like him who have been blessed with stupendous wealth, yet actively share it with humanitarian causes.

I am not afraid to admit that I have a particular affinity with selfless people. I love people who give unselfishly of themselves for others and I love to be in the company of like-minded individuals. I do not get on so well with the person exhibiting the 'me, myself and I' syndrome. Wherever I can, I simply love to add value and I am always keen to use my gifts and talents for worthy causes. This does not mean I am Little Miss Perfect; that is not what I am saying at all. It just means that I have progressed a little further with my evolution as a person.

Ministry began in a library in Battersea and progressed from there to where I am today. Involvement in the ministry has been the bedrock of so many aspects of my life, and one of the most important things is the fact that it made me truly understand the meaning of fulfilment. I realised that life is so much more than work, eat and sleep. To truly live, you must be fulfilled and the sad truth of the matter is that so many people are not.

Fulfilment is not about money or material possessions; it is about waking up with a spring in your step and being happy and grateful to be alive.

My work in ministry also made me realise that many women and young girls suffer from low self-esteem and confidence, which affects their ability to truly fulfil their potential. In ministry, I was surrounded by so many young women who were unhappy that I was inspired to start the social enterprise Proudtobeme, to empower young women via coaching and mentoring, to grow in self-confidence and well-being. I realised that many of the young women I was in contact with reminded me of myself in my younger years. This was a mirror of me; individuals with low confidence, poor self-esteem, always making the wrong choices.

Proudtobeme still exists today and enables me to support young women via inspiring and motivating workshops. We have come a long way from our early days and I am very proud of our achievements, which include collaboration with universities and a steady stream of graduate and postgraduate volunteers.

My journey into coaching was also deeply entrenched in my work in ministry. I am passionate about people and, most importantly, about people fulfilling their destiny and potential. Through this, I established Ebony Business Network, which empowers Black and ethnic minorities to start up and scale up on their entrepreneurial journeys.

In a similar vein, The Women of Destiny is the female arm of the ministry and we exist to embrace women and to assist them on their individual spiritual journeys. We achieve this by organising conferences, events, spa weekends, trips abroad and lunch and breakfast meetings, using our gatherings as an opportunity for fellowship.

It took some time for me to recognise, but I am now firmly convinced that I am destined for the helping professions—as a coach, mentor, trainer, and teacher.

I am a true example that you are constantly on a journey of self-discovery and this journey has nothing to do with age. It is about discovering your truth, listening to your inner voice and finding fulfilment in your work. I am passionate about women and their lives and I want to see them thrive and fulfil their purpose. I am acutely aware of the issues that women face, such as low self-confidence and low self-esteem, and the terrible effect those things can have on their progress and opportunities.

I hope that you will find something in my book to inspire you to fulfil your own dreams in life and arrive at a place where the words 'If She Can, You Can' will turn into 'She did, AND SO DID I!'

# *References*

## Introduction

https://www.scielo.br/scielo.php?pid=S1413-85572020000100324&script=sci_arttext&tlng=en

## Chapter 2

https://www.mentalhealth.org.uk/publications/ impact-traumatic-events-mental-health

# Appendix

## ACAS

- ACAS provides assistance with issues related to employment law and workplace advice for employers, employees, and workers.
    - Monday-Friday 9 am- 5 pm
    - Helpline: 03001231100
    - Using UK text relay: 1800103001231100
    - Email: events@acas.org.uk

## Age UK

- Age UK provides support to the elderly, their families, friends, carers, and professionals by offering reliable and current information.
    - Open every day from 8 am- 7 pm
    - Phone: 08000556112
    - Email: info@agescotland.org.uk

## Asylum Support Appeals Projects (ASAP)

- ASAP offers essential support to individuals facing challenges with asylum support, including accommodation and financial assistance.
    - Mon, Wed, and Fri 2 pm- 4 pm
    - Advice line: 02037160283
    - Email: office@asapprojects.org.uk

## Business Debtline

- Business Debtline offers expert advice on managing business debts, guiding individuals through the process and helping them understand the next steps to take.
    - Mon-Fri 9 am- 8 pm
    - Phone: 08001976026
    - Email: info@businessdebline.org

## Carers UK

- Carers UK is the leading national charity supporting, advocating for, and connecting carers across the UK. The organisation ensures that individuals facing the challenges of caring for a loved one do not have to do so in isolation.
    - Monday-Friday 9 am- 6 pm
    - Phone: 08088087777
    - Email: advice@carersuk.org

## Child Law Advice

- Child Law Advice offers a digital-first service dedicated to providing legal advice and information concerning family, child, and education law to parents, carers, and young people in England.
    - Family line: 03003305480
    - Education line: 03003305485
    - Email: clas@coramclc.org.uk

## Contact a Family

- Contact a Family runs a free advice and information helpline aimed at parents and carers of disabled children aged from birth to 25, living in any part of the UK. This service is dedicated to assisting families in navigating the challenges of raising a disabled child, offering guidance on local support options, preparing for adult life, childcare, education, and learning.
    - Monday-Friday 9:30 am- 5 pm
    - Phone: 08088083555
    - Email: press@contact.org.uk

## Coram Voice

- Coram Voice offers vital independent support to children and young people in Manchester who are in care or have left care.
    - Monday-Friday 9:30 am - 6 pm
    - Phone: +44 (0) 7758670369
    - Email: help@coramvoice.org.uk

## DeafPLUS

- DeafPLUS is a charity dedicated to empowering deaf people and those with hearing impairments, facilitating their ability to live independently. The organisation provides a comprehensive range of services designed to address the unique needs of the deaf and hard of hearing community.
    - Phone: +44 2077906147
    - Email: info@deafplus.org

## Disability Law Service

- Disability Law Service offers crucial support by providing free legal advice in areas critical to the well-being and rights of disabled individuals and their carers.
    - Phone: +44 20 7791 9800
    - Email: advice@dls.org.uk

## Gingerbread

- Gingerbread provides expert advice and information to support all single parents, ensuring they have the tools to support both their children and themselves.
    - Phone: 0808020925
    - Email: campaign@gingerbread.org.uk

## Housing Rights

- Housing Rights advises those facing court for repossession and offers help to those at risk of eviction due to unpaid rent or mortgage.
    - Monday-Friday 9:30 am- 4:30 pm
    - Phone: 02890245640

## Independent Age

- Independent Age helps aid those with the problem of elderly people facing financial hardship. They offer free and impartial advice and information, as well as grants. They highlight the issues experienced by older people who are facing financial insecurity.
    - Phone: 02076054200
    - Email: advice@independentage.org
    - Monday- Friday 9 am- 5 pm

## JCWI (Justice Council for the welfare of immigrants)

- JCWI supports individuals seeking a fulfilling life in the UK by challenging racist and discriminatory policies and educating communities to enhance the lives of people who move or are forced to move.
    - Phone: +44 20 7251 8708
    - Email: press@jcwi.org.uk or press@jcwi.org.uk

## Macmillan Cancer Support

- Macmillan Cancer Support helps raise money to provide vital cancer services, research, and campaigns for better cancer care, and also support the cancer workforce.
    - Open 7 days a week
    - Phone: 2070912230
    - Email: contact@macmillan.org.uk

## Maternity Action

- Maternity Action helps pregnant women and new parents dealing with work-related problems, difficulties accessing maternity pay and benefits, or struggling with the cost of living.
    - Phone: +44 20 72532288
    - Email: media@maternityaction.org.uk or info@maternityaction.org.uk

## Migrant Help UK

- Migrant Help UK provides independent advice and guidance to assist asylum seekers in the UK in navigating and understanding the asylum process.
    - Phone: 08088010503
    - Email: info@migranthelpuk.org

## MIND

- MIND helps and provides support for people in need through housing, crisis helplines, drop-in centres, employment and training schemes, counselling, and befriending.
    - Phone: 03001233393
    - Email: info@mind.org.uk

## National Debtline

- National Debtline is a helpline for people with debt problems. They provide expert advice over the telephone and via email, and offer self-help information to callers.
    - Phone: +44 808 808 4000
    - Email: youraccount@nationaldebtline.org

## National Domestic Violence Helpline

- National Domestic Violence Helpline is run by trained female advisors who help people who have left, still live with, or are planning to leave their abuser. They assist you in understanding what domestic abuse is, your rights and options, how to support a survivor, and how to help yourself if you've been abused.
    - Phone: 808 2000 247
    - No email was found but there are chat services available

## NSPCC

- NSPCC works with children to keep them safe from child abuse. This organization provides support to these children and offers a wide range of services, including helplines, campaigns, and support for families and children.
    - Phone: 08080005000
    - Email: help@NSPCC.org.uk

## Refugee Council

- Refugee Council is a leading charity working with refugees and people seeking asylum in the UK.
- They help those who have fled conflict, violence, and persecution to rebuild their lives in the UK.
    - Phone: 02073466700
    - Email: info@refugeecouncil.org.uk

## Rethink Mental Illness

- Rethink Mental Illness is a leading charity for mental health services, supporting people living with mental illness and their carers. They provide expert advice, information, and around 90 services.
    - Phone: 08008010525
    - Email: advice@rethink.org

## Rights of Women

- Rights of Women provides free confidential legal advice and information to women on the law in England and Wales, with a specific focus on violence against women and girls. They campaign for access to justice and safety for all women.
    - Phone: 02072518887
    - Email: info@row.org.uk

## Royal National Institute of Blind People

- The Royal National Institute of Blind People offers practical and emotional support to blind and partially sighted people, their families, and carers. They raise awareness of the experiences of blind people and campaign to make society more accessible for all.
    - Phone: 02034321488 or 03031239999
    - Email: helpline@rnib.org.uk

## Royal British Legion

- The Royal British Legion provides recovery and rehabilitation support to currently serving and ex-service personnel who are wounded, injured, or sick. This support is also available to those experiencing multiple challenges, such as being out of work, dealing with mental health problems, financial issues, and alcohol abuse.
  - Phone: 08088028080
  - Email: info@britishlegion.org.uk

## Scope

- Scope is a disability equality charity that provides practical information and emotional support when it is most needed. They also campaign to create a fairer society.
  - Phone: 08088003333
  - Email: helpline@scope.org.uk

## Seafarer Support

- Seafarer Support is a helpline run by the Merchant Navy for current and former seafarers and their families, as well as people who work to improve the lives of seafarers and their families.
  - Phone: 08001601842
  - Email: seafarers@itf.org.uk

## Shelter England

- Shelter England provides information and believes that everyone should have a home. They conduct research to understand the UK's housing problems and develop policies to solve them.
  - Monday- Friday 9 am-5 pm
  - Phone: 03003301234
  - Email: info@shelter.org.uk

## StepChange

- StepChange offers free debt advice and money management, aiding those troubled by debt problems and uncertain of their next steps.
  - Monday- Friday 8 am- 8 pm, Saturday 9 am- 2 pm
  - Phone: 08001381111
  - Email: admin.team@stepchange.org

## Taxaid

- TaxAid offers free, independent, and confidential advice to UK tax-payers on a low income who have not been able to sort out their tax issues with HMRC and who are aged 60 or younger or are self-employed.
  - Phone: +44 345 120 3779
  - Monday- Friday 9 am - 5 pm
  - Email: info@taxaid.org.uk

## Veterans Welfare

- Veterans Welfare provides support to veterans and their dependents. The service focuses on assisting with changes in circumstances that may result in welfare needs, such as leaving the services, being discharged, or addressing welfare requirements upon discharge.
    - Monday- Friday 8:30 am- 5 pm
    - Phone: 0808 1914 218
    - Email: veterans-uk@mod.gov.uk

## Working Families

- Working Families' mission is to remove the barriers that people with caring responsibilities face in the workplace. They provide free legal advice to parents and carers on their rights at work.
    - Phone: 0300 012 0312
    - Email: press@workingfamilies.org.uk

# Review Ask

Thank you for reading this book. I hope that you found it useful. If so, please consider leaving a short review on Amazon to help other readers know what the book is about and how it can help them.

If you've enjoyed this journey and would like to share your thoughts, ask questions, or just say hello, I'd love to hear from you. Please feel free to reach out to me at lola@makethatmove.biz

While I strive to read and respond to every message, please forgive any delays due to my writing schedule.

# About the Author

Lola Owolabi, FRSA, FinstLM, MA, is an award-winning coach who helps train new and existing leaders through transformational methods. Lola is also a university tutor who holds a master's degree in coaching from Warwick University. She has inspired, motivated, and mentored women of all ages from various backgrounds via her organisations, Proudtobeme, Ebony Business Network, Women of Destiny and Make That Move Coaching services.

She is passionate about people's creativity and entrepreneurship and is very keen to see people fulfil their potential and unlock all their latent abilities. She has a deep understanding of how low self-esteem and self-doubt can hinder people and thus, her organisations all focus on the boosting of self-esteem and personal wellbeing.

As a creative individual, she has written and co-produced two albums as well as penning three books. She is also the Creative Director/Curator/Coach and Founder of the Wearable Arts Collective (an organisation which focuses on empowering the African creative to take their place on the international stage). Recent fashion shows that her collective has participated in include London Fashion Week and New York Fashion Week in February 2020 (a collaboration with Emerge NYFW).

Lola has recently been appointed as Coach in Residence at York St John University, where she will support students, academic staff, and non-academic staff.

Printed in Great Britain
by Amazon

52181170R00089